"Philip Ryken and Michael LeFebvre have written a delightful book that will help us to better understand the great truth of the Trinity: one God in three Persons. Better yet, it should cause us to grow in our appreciation of the distinct works of Father, Son, and Holy Spirit in our salvation and sanctification. I heartily commend this book."

Jerry Bridges, author, *The Pursuit of Holiness*

"The Westminster Shorter Catechism tells us that 'man's chief end is to glorify God and enjoy him forever.' In this book, the authors bring that affirmation to life by showing us that the Trinity is not just a doctrine to be believed but a relationship to be experienced and enjoyed. Pastors, teachers, and believers everywhere will be refreshed and challenged by this stirring call to a deeper participation in the love of the triune God."

Gerald Bray, Research Professor of Divinity,
Beeson Divinity School

"At a time when biblical theology gets more attention among pastors, the twin advantages of systematic theology—namely that it will hold you to orthodoxy in the face of difficult Biblical texts and that it is organized according to the categories in which the non-Christian world speaks and thinks—cannot be underestimated. With this as the backdrop, Ryken and LeFebvre's *Our Triune God* fills a void in Christian literature. The chapters are formed as carefully reasoned expositions on the subject of the Trinity, and as such, this book provides us with a model worth emulating across the spectrum of systematic categories."

David Helm, Pastor, Holy Trinity Church; Chairman,
Charles Simeon Trust

OUR TRIUNE GOD

OUR TRIUNE GOD

LIVING IN THE LOVE OF THE
THREE-IN-ONE

PHILIP RYKEN
AND
MICHAEL LEFEBVRE

FOREWORD BY ROBERT LETHAM

WHEATON, ILLINOIS

Cover design: Studio Gearbox

Cover photo: Photos.com

First printing 2011

Printed in the United States of America

Italics in biblical quotes indicate emphasis added.

Unless otherwise indicated, Scripture quotations are from the ESV® Bible (*The Holy Bible, English Standard Version*®), copyright © 2001 by Crossway. Used by permission. All rights reserved.

ISBN-13: 978-1-4335-1987-1
ISBN-10: 1-4335-1987-9
PDF ISBN: 978-1-4335-1988-8
Mobipocket ISBN: 978-1-4335-1989-5
ePub ISBN: 978-1-4335-1990-1

Library of Congress Cataloging-in-Publication Data
Ryken, Philip Graham, 1966–
  Our triune God : living in the love of the triune God / Philip
Graham Ryken and Michael LeFebvre.
    p. cm.
Includes bibliographical references and index.
  ISBN-13: 978-1-4335-1987-1 (tpb)   ISBN-10: 1-4335-1987-9
  ISBN-13: 978-1-4335-1988-8 (PDF)
  ISBN-13: 978-1-4335-1989-5 (Mobipocket)
  1. Trinity. I. LeFebvre, Michael. II. Title.
BT111.3.R95   2011
231'.044—dc22   2010023931

Crossway is a publishing ministry of Good News Publishers.

VP		20	19	18	17	16	15	14	13	12	11
14	13	12	11	10	9	8	7	6	5	4	3	2	1

In memory of
Bud Wilson

CONTENTS

FOREWORD

✠

It should be obvious that at the center of Christianity is the worship of God. It is from this, glorifying God and enjoying him now and forever, that the Christian life and its various outworkings proceed. The supreme biblical revelation of God is that he is triune—he is the Father, the Son, and the Holy Spirit, three Persons in indivisible union. The Trinitarian baptismal formula (Matt. 28:19–20) is pronounced over everyone who can be called a Christian.

Yet in the Western church the doctrine of the Trinity has been greatly neglected. For most Christians it is little more than an arcane mystery, of little significance for everyday life. While it may be believed, our knowledge of God is strangely disconnected from the reality of his tri-personal being.

Recent decades have seen a recovery of interest in the Trinity at the academic, theological level. What is vitally needed is for this to percolate through to the pew. Once it does it will transform our faith and shed light on a vast range of areas, while both stimulating and enhancing evangelism.

This book is exactly what is required. Philip Ryken and Michael LeFebvre present this most mysterious and yet crucial truth in a compelling way that should be enlightening to a wide readership. They are faithful to the truth and attuned to the questions raised by believers and unbelievers alike. Their presentation is lucid and readable without cutting corners or sacrificing principles. There is much wise biblical exposition, and the context of worship is persistently stressed, but the authors do not shirk the difficult questions and do interact with the theories of relativity and quantum mechanics and with Islam. If you are looking to grow in your knowledge of God and want a straightforward but intelligent guide to the Trinity, look no further—this is it.

I am delighted to commend this volume and pray that it may be instrumental in stimulating the faith, understanding, worship, and Christian lives of all who read it.

Robert Letham

INTRODUCTION

God is one; . . . this one God is Father, Son, and
Holy Ghost; . . . the Father is the Father of the Son;
and the Son, the Son of the Father; and the Holy Ghost,
the Spirit of the Father and the Son; and . . . in
respect of this their mutual relations,
they are distinct from each other. (John Owen)[1]

✛

To know God is to know him as triune. There is one God in three Persons. Or to express the same truth in a different way, God is three Persons in one being—Father, Son, and Holy Spirit.

This Trinitarian truth is foundational to the worship and the service of God. To know God as triune is to worship him as he is, rejoicing in his very being. We praise the Father, the Son, and the Holy Spirit for having equal, divine majesty, while at the same time honoring each Person's unique personality: the Father is the Father of the Son; the Son is the Son of the Father; the Spirit is sent by the Father and the Son. Out of this worship comes our service, as we show the Father's mercy and proclaim the Son's sacrifice in the power of the Holy Spirit.

Historically, the church has placed great importance on the doctrine of the Trinity, which has been held universally across the church and around the world. The early church father Irenaeus claimed that apart from the reality of the Trinity we cannot know God at all: "Without the Spirit it is not possible to behold the [Son] of God, nor without the Son can any draw near the Father: for the knowledge of the Father is the Son, and the knowledge of the Son of God is through the Holy Spirit; and, according to the

[1]William H. Goold, *The Works of John Owen* (Edinburgh: Banner of Truth, 1980), 2.377.

good pleasure of the Father, the Son ministers and dispenses the Spirit to whomsoever the Father wills and as He wills."[2]

The same Trinitarian doctrine is clearly confessed in the ancient creeds of the Christian church. In the Apostles' Creed, for example, believers confess their faith in "God, the Father Almighty," in "Jesus Christ, his only Son, our Lord," and in "the Holy Ghost." Similarly, the Nicene Creed states, "I believe in God the Father Almighty, Maker of heaven and earth . . . and in Jesus Christ, the only-begotten Son of God . . . and in the Holy Ghost, the Lord and Giver of life, who proceedeth from the Father and the Son, who with the Father and the Son together is worshipped and glorified."

The Trinity was strongly reaffirmed by the Reformers, believing as they did that the doctrine was plainly taught in Scripture. Like many Christians, Martin Luther found it hard to understand how one God could exist in three Persons, yet had to affirm what he read in God's Word. Luther said, "Since I see that it is so distinctly contained and grounded in Scripture, I believe God more than my own thoughts and reason and do not worry about how it can possibly be true that there is only one Essence and yet that there are three distinct Persons in this one Essence: God the Father, God the Son, and God the Holy Ghost."[3] Similarly, John Calvin exhorted the readers of his famous *Institutes* to know God in the fullness of his triune majesty: "God . . . proclaims himself the sole God . . . to be contemplated clearly in Three Persons. Unless we grasp these, only the bare and empty name of God flits about in our brains, to the exclusion of the true God."[4]

Sad to say, although the church has long cherished this doctrine, a very different attitude has emerged in recent centuries. The eighteenth-century Enlightenment launched an era of height-

---

[2]Irenaeus, *Dem. ap.* 7. Translation from *St. Irenaeus: The Demonstration of the Apostolic Preaching*, trans. J. Armitage Robinson (London: SPCK, 1920), 76.
[3]Martin Luther, *What Luther Says: A Practical In-Home Anthology for the Active Christian*, ed. Ewald M. Plass (Saint Louis: Concordia, 1959), 1388–1389.
[4]John Calvin, *Institutes of the Christian Religion*, trans. Ford Lewis Battles, 2 vols., Library of Christian Classics, 20–21 (Philadelphia: Westminster, 1960), I.xiii.2.

ened rationalism in the West. Human reason came to be viewed as the ultimate standard for determining truth. According to the spirit of the age, doctrines marked by a supernatural character tended to be pushed to the sidelines. The mysterious doctrine of the Trinity was an early casualty of modernist rationalism, for who can comprehend the idea of one indivisible being existing in three distinct Persons?

Friedrich Schleiermacher's influential book *The Christian Faith*, first published in 1821, illustrates this new attitude toward Trinitarianism. In his summary of Christian doctrine, Schleiermacher left the subject of the Trinity to a few paragraphs at the very end of the book. The doctrine was more like an afterthought than a prominent focus of his thinking. This is a very different priority than that found in Calvin's *Institutes of the Christian Religion* (1536), in which the Genevan Reformer placed an entire chapter on the Trinity in his first volume.

The difference between Calvin and Schleiermacher illustrates the unfortunate shift that has occurred. The contemporary church has largely forgotten the importance of knowing God as triune. Granted, most children who grow up in the church today are taught in Sunday school that God is three in one—Father, Son, and Holy Spirit. But Christians are rarely encouraged to think deeply about the Trinity or to make God's triune being the focus of their worship and service to God. This detrimental trend needs to be corrected, and the present book is offered to address that need by helping Christians grow in their relationship to God in his triunity.

The approach we take is not only theological but also biblical, and therefore practical. Chapter 1 ("The Saving Trinity") looks at the book of Ephesians, where the apostle Paul teaches us to think about our salvation in Trinitarian terms. Salvation is not the work of a flat, nondimensional deity; rather, salvation is the glorious work of the cooperative majesty of the triune God. To know and to praise God as our Savior is to love him as the Trinity.

Chapter 2 ("The Mysterious Trinity") considers some of the questions that make the Trinity hard to comprehend. People sometimes wonder whether it is even reasonable to believe in a God who is three in one. Moreover, they wonder how to relate the Old Testament emphasis on monotheism with New Testament teachings on God's triune nature. Rather than confusing us, these points of intellectual challenge should be part of our thoughtful reverence—loving God with all our minds.

Chapter 3 ("The Practical Trinity") focuses on John 13–17, where Jesus teaches his disciples to relate to God as triune. Far from treating the subject as an intellectual discourse, Jesus shows the practicality of this doctrine for shaping our daily relationship with God as Father, Son, and Holy Spirit.

The final chapter ("The Joyous Trinity") explores a series of passages in Luke where the cooperation of all three Persons is described. Luke's reporting on the Trinity in these texts displays the power and joy that God has within himself and intends to share with us as we know him in his triune being and action.

The present volume is not a historical theology of Trinitarianism. It is designed instead to help Christians grow in their personal relationship with God as triune, and we pray that the Lord will bless it to that end.

There is an intentional focus throughout on the individual Christian and his or her personal relationship with God. Another volume would be needed to address the subject of the church's relationship to the triune God corporately—in congregational worship, body life, and corporate acts of service. Nevertheless, the church's communal service for God together is an outgrowth of knowing God as individual believers. So our personal relationship with the Trinity is an important starting point.

Something else this book does not include is a history of the church's debates over the doctrine of the Trinity, as valuable as such a history would be. The church's delight in the Trinity has many exciting chapters, worthy of study and attention. Beginning with the apostles, early Christian missionaries went throughout the world planting new churches in the name of the triune God, as Jesus had commanded: "Go therefore and make disciples of all nations, baptizing them in the name of the Father and of the Son and of the Holy Spirit" (Matt. 28:19). While expanding into new lands over many centuries, the church has continued to treasure the doctrine of the Trinity. Many false teachings emerged over time as well, including heresies that persist today (for example, the Jehovah's Witnesses hold views of Christ similar to those condemned when the third-century church confronted the teachings of Arius). Other books will prove worthwhile for readers who are interested in learning more about the history of this doctrine and the heresies that arose against it. We particularly recommend Robert Letham's book, *The Holy Trinity: In Scripture, History, Theology, and Worship.*

The main chapters in this volume began as talks delivered to the 2007 Conference of the Reformation Society of Indiana, which was hosted by the Second Reformed Presbyterian Church of Indianapolis. Carlisle "Bud" Wilson was the enthusiastic visionary not only for that conference but also for many other initiatives over the years aimed at promoting Reformation theology, including the formation of the Society itself.

Unbeknownst to us at the time, the Autumn 2007 conference was to be the last that Bud would organize. On March 19, 2008, after many years of faithful service to his beloved Savior Jesus Christ, leaning on the power of the Holy Spirit, for the glory of God the Father, Bud entered the presence of his triune God. With thanksgiving to the Father, the Son, and the Holy Spirit for his ministry, this volume is dedicated to the memory of Bud Wilson (1932–2008), with appreciation for his wife, Marty.

1

THE SAVING TRINITY

OUR TRIUNE GOD AND THE PLAN OF SALVATION

*Grace to you and peace from God our Father and the
Lord Jesus Christ. . . . In him you also, when you heard
the word of truth, the gospel of your salvation,
and believed in him, were sealed with the promised
Holy Spirit. (Eph. 1:2, 13)*

*To the great One in Three
Eternal praises be,
Hence evermore.
His sovereign majesty
May we in glory see,
And to eternity
Love and adore.
(Anonymous; eighteenth century)*

A good place to begin knowing the triune God is at the very
beginning, which is where Ephesians 1 begins. Before we were
born—before anyone was born—before God made the heavens
and the earth, even before the angels first praised their Maker,
God was planning to save his people from their sins. We were
destined to salvation long ages before the world was ever created.
This was the work of the triune God.

The plan of salvation required the active engagement of every

Person of the Trinity: Father, Son, and Spirit. Therefore, in the opening chapter of Ephesians, the apostle Paul praises first the Father (vv. 3–6), then the Son (vv. 7–12), and finally the Holy Spirit (vv. 13–14) for the part each plays in salvation. Salvation is administered by the Father, accomplished by the Son, and applied by the Spirit. The mystery at the epicenter of the universe—namely, the triune being of God—is also the heart of our salvation. Our redemption is Trinitarian in its structure.

THE THREE-PERSONED GOD

It is sometimes thought that because the term *Trinity* does not appear in Scripture, the doctrine is unbiblical, or at least irrelevant. One famous critic was the German philosopher Immanuel Kant, who claimed that "the doctrine of the Trinity, taken literally, has *no practical relevance at all*, even if we think we understand it; and it is even more clearly irrelevant if we realize that it transcends all our concepts" (emphasis in the original).[5] It is true that the biblical doctrine of the Trinity is mysterious. It is such a great mystery, in fact, that we may never be able fully to understand it, let alone explain it. One thing we must do, however, is to believe in the Trinity, for in his perfect Word God has revealed himself as one God in three Persons. The true God is a triunity.

For all its complexity, the biblical doctrine of the Trinity can be stated in seven simple propositions:

1. God the Father is God.
2. God the Son is God.
3. God the Holy Spirit is God.
4. The Father is not the Son.
5. The Son is not the Spirit.
6. The Spirit is not the Father.
7. Nevertheless, there is only one God.

---

[5]Immanuel Kant, *The Conflict of the Faculties*, trans. Mary J. Gregor (New York: Abaris, 1979), 65.

This is the doctrine of the Trinity, stated in propositional form, as distilled from Scripture. In his treatise *On Christian Doctrine*, Augustine used somewhat different language to express the same eternal truths:

> The Father and the Son and the Holy Spirit, and each of these by Himself, is God, and at the same time they are all one God. . . . The Father is not the Son nor the Holy Spirit; the Son is not the Father nor the Holy Spirit; the Holy Spirit is not the Father nor the Son: but the Father is only Father, the Son is only Son, and the Holy Spirit is only Holy Spirit.[6]

THE TRIUNE GOD WHO SAVES

Ephesians 1 brings these bare propositions to life, for it shows the triune God working out our salvation. The Trinity is not an abstraction but a living, working, Creator-Redeemer. God is who he is in his triune being for our salvation. We are chosen by God the Father, in Christ the Son, through God the Holy Spirit. Or, as we have already noted, salvation is *administered* by the Father, *accomplished* by the Son, and *applied* by the Spirit. To express the same truths in yet another way, the salvation that was *planned* by the Father has been *procured* by the Son and is now *presented* and *protected* by the Spirit. Whatever words we use to describe it, the point is that our salvation from sin depends on a gracious cooperation within the Godhead.

Nearly the whole first chapter of Ephesians is one long sentence in the original Greek. As the apostle Paul began his letter to the church in Ephesus, he was overwhelmed by God's grace in salvation. So he wrote, "Blessed be the God and Father of our Lord Jesus Christ, who has blessed us in Christ with every spiritual blessing in the heavenly places" (Eph. 1:3). Then Paul proceeded to praise God for all the blessings of salvation, which takes a while, and the apostle did not stop until he was finished.

---

[6]Augustine, *On Christian Doctrine*, ed. Philip Schaff, *Nicene and Post-Nicene Fathers*, First Series (1887; repr. Peabody, MA: Hendrickson, 1995), I.5 (2:524).

The long sentence that runs from Ephesians 1:3 to Ephesians 1:14 stretches from eternity to eternity, showing the full saving work of the triune God. It lays out the whole scope of salvation, the plan that God has been working on forever. Our salvation began in the mind of God before the beginning of time, when our God and Father planned to save a people for himself. He planned to adopt us as his own sons and daughters. He planned to redeem us from our sins by sending a Savior, his own Son, Jesus Christ. He planned to sanctify us, to make us holy. Finally, God planned to bring us to glory.

What a great plan! The late James Montgomery Boice summarized it by comparing it to music:

> This story has three movements, like a symphony. The first movement is the sovereign election of God according to which he has chosen to bless a special people with every possible spiritual blessing in his Son Jesus Christ. The second movement is the accomplishing of that purpose through the redeeming death of Jesus. . . . The final movement . . . concerns the work of the Holy Spirit by which those who have been chosen by the Father and redeemed by the Lord Jesus Christ are actually "linked up" to salvation.[7]

God plays the symphony of our salvation in three movements. Each movement is associated with a different Person of the Trinity: the Father, the Son, and the Holy Spirit. First, there is the work of God the Father in administering our salvation. The Father is the one who organizes and oversees the plan of salvation. Second, there is the work of God the Son in accomplishing our salvation. Jesus is the one who died on the cross for our sins and rose again to give us eternal life. Third, there is the work of God the Holy Spirit in applying our salvation. The Spirit is the one who takes what Jesus Christ has done and makes it ours. This is the plan, and the triune God has been working it out since before the beginning of time.

---

[7]James Montgomery Boice, *Ephesians* (Grand Rapids, MI: Baker, 1988, 1997), 28.

SALVATION IN THREE MOVEMENTS

Salvation starts with the Father, who is the origination of our salvation:

> Blessed be the God and Father of our Lord Jesus Christ, who has blessed us in Christ with every spiritual blessing in the heavenly places, even as he chose us in him before the foundation of the world, that we should be holy and blameless before him. In love he predestined us for adoption as sons through Jesus Christ, according to the purpose of his will, to the praise of his glorious grace, with which he has blessed us in the Beloved. (Eph. 1:3–6)

The Father deliberately blesses, chooses, and predestines his people. He lovingly bestows, reveals, and lavishes his grace. This is all part of the eternal plan of the one who "works all things according to the counsel of his will" (Eph. 1:11).

The salvation that originated with the Father is located in the Son. The opening verses of Ephesians focus their attention on the person and work of Jesus Christ, mentioning his person and work no fewer than a dozen times. Although the passage as a whole is Trinitarian in its structure, there is special focus on Christ as Savior. Everything God does (and has done and will do) for our salvation, he does in Christ:

> In him we have redemption through his blood, the forgiveness of our trespasses, according to the riches of his grace, which he lavished upon us, in all wisdom and insight making known to us the mystery of his will, according to his purpose, which he set forth in Christ as a plan for the fullness of time, to unite all things in him, things in heaven and things on earth. In him we have obtained an inheritance, having been predestined according to the purpose of him who works all things according to the counsel of his will, so that we who were the first to hope in Christ might be to the praise of his glory. (Eph. 1:7–12)

By listing so many benefits of salvation, these verses set the agenda for the Bible's saving message. Salvation means election, God's choice to save us by his predestinating grace (Eph. 1:4–5). Salvation means redemption, the payment of a price to free us from our bondage to sin (Eph. 1:7). Salvation means adoption, the legal act by which God makes us his own sons and daughters (Eph. 1:5). Salvation means propitiation, the atoning blood sacrifice that takes away our guilt and secures our forgiveness (Eph. 1:7). Salvation means reconciliation, on a cosmic scale, for in Christ God is unifying everything in the universe (Eph. 1:10). Christ's reconciling work operates horizontally as well as vertically; it is for the Jews ("we who were the first to hope in Christ," Eph. 1:12) and also for the Gentiles ("you also, when you heard the word of truth," Eph. 1:13). Thus reconciliation ends both our alienation from God and our estrangement from one another. Salvation means, finally, sanctification and glorification, in which God makes us as morally spotless and as shiningly beautiful as his own dear Son (Eph. 1:12).

These verses contain virtually the whole message of salvation, which Paul describes as "the mystery of [God's] will" (Eph. 1:9). This saving message communicates that all of God's best blessings come through union with Jesus Christ. This is how we come into full relationship with the triune God: we are blessed with every spiritual blessing "*in Christ*" (Eph. 1:3). Just as we were utterly lost in Adam, through the imputation of his sin, so we are completely saved in Christ, through the gift of his salvation. In Christ we are predestined, redeemed, forgiven, adopted, reconciled, sanctified, and glorified. Christ is not only the beginning and the end of our salvation, he *is* our salvation, for in him we receive everything we need to be saved. The location of our salvation is Jesus Christ.

The salvation that originated with the Father and is located in the Son is communicated by the Holy Spirit. Or as we expressed it earlier, salvation is administered by God the Father, accomplished by God the Son, and applied by God the Spirit: "In him you also, when you heard the word of truth, the gospel of your salvation, and believed in him, were sealed with the promised Holy Spirit, who is the guarantee of our inheritance until we acquire possession of it, to the praise of his glory" (Eph. 1:13–14).

Since God's best blessings are spiritual, we can receive them only by his Spirit. First the Holy Spirit enables us to hear the gospel of truth, which is the message of salvation. Then he changes us from the inside out, the gracious act also known as regeneration. With regeneration comes the gift of faith, the spiritual ability to believe in the death and resurrection of Jesus Christ. By doing this work in us, the Holy Spirit makes our salvation a present reality. He takes the salvation that the Son accomplished in the past and applies it to us in the present. It is for this reason that the Holy Spirit is called a "seal" (Eph. 1:13), which in ancient times was proof of ownership. The sealing work of the Holy Spirit proves that we really do belong to God and will continue to belong to him for all eternity. Hence the Spirit is also called an advance "guarantee" or deposit (Eph. 1:14). In the spiritual transaction God has made with us, the Holy Spirit is a down payment on eternity, the security of our salvation, now and forever.

The first half of Ephesians 1 gives a complete overview of the work of the triune God in saving sinners. All the blessings of salvation come from God, in Christ, by the Holy Spirit. Our salvation jointly depends on the electing, predestining work of God the Father; the redeeming, atoning work of God the Son; and the sealing, guaranteeing work of God the Holy Spirit.[8] Anyone who admits the need for salvation can see why the doctrine of the Trinity is so important and so practical. Not only is the existence of one God in three Persons central to our worship, but it is also central for our salvation.

One of the most careful explanations of the doctrine of the Trinity comes from the Athanasian Creed, which was written

---

[8] See Eric J. Alexander, "The Basis of Christian Salvation," in *Faithful Witness*, ed. James McLeish (Downers Grove, IL: InterVarsity, 1985), 30.

around AD 400. First the creed states the doctrine: "There is one Person of the Father: another of the Son: and another of the Holy Ghost. But the Godhead of the Father, of the Son, and of the Holy Ghost, is all one. . . . The Father eternal: the Son eternal: and the Holy Ghost eternal. And yet they are not three eternals: but one eternal." That is the doctrine, but the Athanasian Creed goes on to explain why it matters: "He therefore that will be saved, must thus think of the Trinity."[9] The message of salvation by grace depends upon the threefold work of the triune God.

BEFORE THE FOUNDATION OF THE WORLD

God's saving work began in eternity past. The emphasis in Ephesians 1 is not so much on the Spirit's application of salvation in the present, or even on the Son's accomplishment of salvation in the past, but on the Father's administration of salvation before the beginning of time. Our salvation was predestined, for we were chosen before the creation of the world (Eph. 1:4–5). The saving work of Jesus Christ in history thus depends on the saving plan of God from all eternity. To understand salvation, we need to go back with the Trinity all the way to eternity past.

It is becoming increasingly popular for theologians (including some who call themselves evangelicals) to think of God as performing without a script. They say that God is "in process." In other words, like the rest of us, he is working things out as he goes along, suffering the vicissitudes of life in this universe and changing his plans to fit the circumstances. In this view, there is a creative interchange between earth and heaven that allows human beings to influence God, even to change his mind altogether. God is not sovereign; he is a finite being who does not fully know the future, although he is open to the possibilities.[10]

---

[9]"The Athanasian Creed," in *The Creeds of Christendom; Volume II: The Greek and Latin Creeds*, ed. Philip Schaff, rev. David S. Schaff, 6th edition, 3 vols. (New York, 1931; repr. Grand Rapids, MI: Baker, 1993), 3:66–71.

[10]This view has been advocated, for example, in Clark H. Pinnock, *A Wideness in God's Mercy: The Finality of Jesus Christ in a World of Religions* (Grand Rapids, MI: Zondervan,

This is not the biblical picture of the triune God. It is true, of course, that God is actively at work in human history. He blesses the righteous and curses the wicked. He answers prayers, converts sinners, and plants churches. He rules over nature and the nations. But God does all these things strictly according to the plan he established before he created the world. God's participation in history depends on his purpose in eternity. He is working everything out according to his eternal plan, a Trinitarian plan that predates the creation of the universe.

In one sense, all God's plans were established in eternity. The Bible could hardly be stronger on this point than it is: we are "predestined according to the purpose of him who works all things according to the counsel of his will" (Eph. 1:11). What is included in God's eternal decree? Everything that God has ever done and everything that he will ever do. This verse uses three different Greek words to describe God's plan. One is the word *thelema*, which simply refers to God's "will" in general. Another is the word *prothesis*, which means God's "purpose," especially his foreordained purpose. The third is the word *boule*, which refers to God's deliberate "counsel." Taken together, these words show that nothing lies outside the divine intention. God does whatever he does according to his predetermined plan.

If God works out *everything* according to his eternal decree, then his eternal decree must include the plan of salvation. This is specifically what is meant by predestination ("In love he predestined us," Eph. 1:4–5). Predestination is one special part of God's cosmic plan. It is his sovereign decision, made in eternity past, regarding the final destiny of individual sinners.

Divine election proves beyond all question or doubt that salvation is by grace alone. Salvation cannot depend on anything we do because we were predestined to it before we ever did anything, even before we existed. The salvation we possess in the present,

1992) and Gregory A. Boyd, *God of the Possible: A Biblical Introduction to the Open View of God* (Grand Rapids, MI: Baker, 2000).

which gives us certain hope for the future, depends on a decision God made in the eternal past.

KNOWING FOR SURE

Election is a glorious doctrine; yet it makes some people uneasy because it naturally causes them to wonder whether they are predestined or not. Indeed, some people experience high anxiety because they fear they are *not* among the elect. Their question becomes, how can I know if God has chosen me or not? It is a reasonable question. If salvation depends on election, then it would seem that being sure of my salvation requires being sure of my election.

How then can we be sure that we are among God's elect? The answer lies in the triune being of God. Here it helps to remember that the elect are chosen *in Christ*. Election in Christ is the only kind of election there is. What God has chosen to do is to unite us to Christ, putting us together with him for our salvation. Therefore, to ask if we are among the elect is really to ask if we are in Christ. If we want to know whether or not God has chosen us, all we need to know is whether or not we are in Christ. We do not need to read God's mind. We do not need to climb up to heaven and peek into the Book of Life. The triune God has made himself known to us in Christ. So all we need to know is Jesus Christ, who is the location of salvation. Every spiritual blessing God has to offer may be found in him, including election. If we are in Christ, therefore, we are among the elect, for the elect are chosen in Christ. John Calvin thus warned that "if we have been elected in him [Christ], we shall not find assurance of election in ourselves." Rather, Christ "is the mirror wherein we must, and without self-deception may, contemplate our own election."[11] The way to make our calling and election sure is to be sure that we are joined to Jesus Christ by faith.

[11]John Calvin, *Institutes of the Christian Religion*, ed. John T. McNeill, trans. Ford Lewis Battles, 2 vols., Library of Christian Classics, 20–21 (Philadelphia: Westminster, 1960), III. xxiv.5.

Since election is in Christ, it is usually best understood after one becomes a Christian. In fact, the doctrine of election is sometimes referred to as a "family secret" (although it is not really a secret to anyone who knows the Bible). While we are still outside God's family, we may not hear about predestination at all; if we do, it hardly seems to make any sense. Once we are in the family, however, it makes the most perfect sense in the world. Indeed, it is the kind of fact that helps us make sense of everything else.

The famous American Bible teacher and evangelist Donald Grey Barnhouse often used an illustration to help people make sense of election. He asked them to imagine a cross like the cross on which Jesus died, only so large that it had a door in it. Over the door were these words from Revelation: "Whosoever will may come" (22:17). These words represent the free and universal offer of the gospel. By God's grace, the message of salvation is for everyone. Every man, woman, and child who will come to the cross is invited to believe in Jesus Christ and so enter eternal life.

On the other side of the door a happy surprise awaits the one who believes and enters. For from the inside, anyone glancing back can see these words from Ephesians written above the door: "Chosen in Christ before the foundation of the world" (1:4). Election is best understood in hindsight, for it is only after coming to Christ that we can look and know that we have been chosen in Christ. Those who make a decision for Christ find that the triune God made a decision for them in eternity past. In the words of an anonymous hymn from the nineteenth century,

> I sought the Lord, and afterward I knew
> He moved my soul to seek him, seeking me;
> It was not I that found, O Savior true;
> No, I was found of thee.

THE SEAL OF OUR SALVATION

Salvation does not come from the sinner's own choice but from God's sovereign choosing. This choice is confirmed by the ministry of the Holy Spirit, who is the seal of salvation.

The importance of having the right seal may be illustrated from the experience of two high school students on a mission trip to Haiti. The boys arrived at the airport in Port-au-Prince—one runway, one small building, and one long line through Immigration. As they approached the customs agent, it was obvious that there was a problem. The man ahead of them in line had a passport and also a birth certificate, as the Haitians require. However, the customs agent kept running her fingers over the corner of the document and complaining about something.

Even with their limited French, the high school students could tell what was happening. The customs agent was trying to feel the raised imprint of a seal—a seal that would prove the document's authenticity. But the birth certificate was only a photocopy, and since it was not marked with a seal, the official was threatening to deny the man entrance to her country.

Suddenly one of the two students said with dismay, "All I have is a copy. What if they don't let me in?" His friend's fingers instinctively moved to the corner of his own birth certificate. Feeling the place where it was certified, he was reassured to know that he had the document he needed: it was marked with a seal. At that moment his friend would have given anything to have the assurance that he would get where he wanted to go (even though, in the end, he was admitted to the country).

If we are wise we will have the same concern about our entrance to the kingdom of heaven. Do you know where you are going, and are you sure that God will let you into his heaven? Do you have the right credentials? Have you received the proper documentation?

The seal of God's salvation is the Holy Spirit. Ephesians 1 begins at the beginning, but it also ends at the end, with the great day when all God's people will enter the fair country of heaven. How do we know for sure that God will let us in? We can only have complete assurance of our salvation if we have been marked with the seal of God's approval: "In him you also, when you heard the word of truth, the gospel of your salvation, and believed in him, were sealed with the promised Holy Spirit, who is the guarantee of our inheritance until we acquire possession of it, to the praise of his glory" (Eph. 1:13–14). The Holy Spirit is the seal of salvation. Everyone who has the Spirit has received a down payment on eternity.

As soon as we start thinking about eternity, we may well begin to get uneasy. How can we possibly wrap our minds around an infinite God? It is the kind of question that keeps a child awake at night, thinking about forever. The questions raised by eternity are not merely theoretical but also intensely practical: What's going to happen to me? How can I know for sure that God will save me at the very end?

To ask the same question another way, what is going to happen when we die? This is a question most people do not like to think about very much, but they ought to. It is good for us to face up to the reality of death. One Dutch grandmother used to go out into a cornfield to inspect her tombstone. When her husband died, she had her own name engraved on the stone at the same time. It was cheaper that way, so it appealed to her native sense of frugality. It was also good for her spiritually, because it helped her prepare to die. Whenever she went to visit her husband's grave, she would see her own name there, with her date of birth, followed by a dash. All that was missing was her date of death.

But what happens then? What happens when we die? Someone will dig a hole in the ground, put our body into it, and let it return to dust. If anyone is going to save us at that point, it is going to have to be God, because no one else can raise the dead. So the question returns with personal intensity: How can I know for sure? How can I know that God has chosen me for salvation?

How can I know that God will save me on the last day and raise me to everlasting life—body and soul?

To answer this question we do not have to go back and read the Father's mind. We do not have to climb up into heaven and peek in the Book of Life. We do not have to be able to tell the future. All we need to do is know Jesus Christ, because when we believe in him for our salvation, God seals us with his Spirit. The same Triune God who made his plans in the past and who controls the future is working in our lives right now by the Holy Spirit, who bears inward witness that we really are the children of God (see Rom. 8:15). The seal of God's Spirit is the guarantee of eternal life.

When does God fix his seal on someone? This happens when we believe in Jesus Christ. The Scripture says, "In him you also, when you heard the word of truth, the gospel of your salvation, and believed in him, were sealed with the promised Holy Spirit" (Eph. 1:13).

What the Scripture says here is true of every Christian. There was a time when we were not included, when we did not know Christ. We were living for ourselves. We were without God and without hope in the world. We probably did not even realize that we were sinners in need of salvation. But then we came to know Jesus Christ in a saving way. We were included in Christ.

It is always nice to be included. No one likes to be left out. But of all the places to be included, this is absolutely the most important—to be included in Christ, to belong to him, so that we have a piece of everything he has to offer. Theologians call this connection "union with Christ." It simply means that when we believe in Christ, we really are joined to him in a spiritual way. We participate in him spiritually, and therefore we have a part in everything he did for our salvation.

Everyone who gets into Christ by faith is marked with a seal, the promised Holy Spirit. This is how the triune God brings his saving work to its secure conclusion. God's seal is invisible.

Because he is spirit, no one can see God. But he is really there. God the Holy Spirit is present in the mind and heart of every Christian.

The Holy Spirit is not only present, but he is also active. He is hard at work bringing the life of God into the soul of every man, woman, and child who believes in Jesus Christ. The Holy Spirit first brings us to the place where we hear the word of truth. As we hear this saving word, the Holy Spirit convinces us that we are sinners in need of a Savior and enables us to trust in the good news about Jesus Christ. He testifies to our minds and hearts that the Bible really is the Word of God, which has the power to save us. Afterward the Holy Spirit disturbs our conscience when we wander away from God. He also enables us to call God "Father." This is all the work of the Holy Spirit, who secures our salvation by sealing us for God.

The Holy Spirit is sometimes considered the forgotten member of the Trinity. But this is because the Holy Spirit is always directing our attention to the Son and thereby fulfilling the Father's plan of salvation. How wonderful it is that the Holy Spirit does this work! Jesus Christ accomplished our salvation two thousand years ago, but by the presence of his Spirit, God brings Christ to us right here and right now. If we know Jesus Christ in a saving way, God is working in us to secure our salvation. This work is too important to entrust to anyone else, so God comes and does it himself. The indwelling Holy Spirit is the seal of the triune God in the soul of every Christian—God's own work in our lives.

The Spirit's work means that our ongoing salvation does not depend on us. Rather, it depends on God's work in us. This is vitally important because our feelings tend to fluctuate. Sometimes we feel more spiritual, while sometimes we do not feel very spiritual at all. In fact, sometimes we wonder whether we even belong to Christ. If our salvation depended on us, then we would be about as stable as the stock market. But our salvation depends on God's Spirit, who is the seal of our salvation. The Spirit makes our salvation secure, like the seal on the back of a letter. John Calvin wrote, "The true conviction which believers have of the Word of God, of their own salvation, and of all religion, does not spring from the feeling of the flesh, or from human and philosophical arguments, but from the sealing of the Spirit, who makes their consciences more certain."[12] If we are having doubts about our salvation, this is only natural. What we need is the *super*natural work of God's Holy Spirit.

A DOWN PAYMENT ON ETERNITY

In the ancient world seals were used to mark official documents, the same way they are used today on charters and diplomas. A legal paper would be drawn up, sealed with wax, and then impressed with some official insignia, perhaps using a signet ring. One document that would have been sealed like this was a last will and testament. Perhaps this explains why the apostle Paul went on to describe the Holy Spirit as "the guarantee of our inheritance until we acquire possession of it" (Eph. 1:14).

This verse mentions at least two things the Holy Spirit does for every believer: he guarantees our inheritance, and he proves that we belong to God. First, he guarantees our inheritance. The Holy Spirit is God's deposit on our salvation. A deposit is a kind of promise or pledge. When someone puts down a deposit, as on a house, they are promising in good faith that they will pay the full asking price at some later date. They are not paying the whole amount immediately, but they put down a deposit to show that they are serious about making the purchase.

To put this in spiritual terms, when God sends us his Spirit, he is making a down payment on eternity. The Holy Spirit is God's way of promising us that more is on the way. One day God will give us the rest of what we have coming to us—all the blessings

---

[12]John Calvin, *Commentaries on Galatians and Ephesians*, trans. William Pringle (Grand Rapids, MI: Baker Books, 1999), 208.

of salvation. He will raise us from the dead. He will take us to heaven and give us the full joy of being with him forever. The Spirit's present work in our lives is a sign of our full and future salvation. Whatever present experience we have of the Holy Spirit, however incomplete it may be, is a promise of eternal life. The Bible says, "He who has prepared us for this very thing is God, who has given us the Spirit as a guarantee" (2 Cor. 5:5; cf. 2 Cor. 1:22).

Remember that a deposit is actually part of the payment. It's the first installment. When people hand over a deposit, they are not just promising to pay later; they are starting to pay right away. They are paying part of the purchase price in advance. Charles Hodge thus defined a deposit as "part of the price of anything purchased, paid as a security for the full payment."[13]

When God gives us his Spirit, therefore, he is doing more than merely promising something later. Since he is a deposit, the Holy Spirit is actually part of our inheritance, the first installment of our heavenly reward. Usually we have to wait until somebody dies to get our inheritance, but as Christians we can begin to enjoy ours right away, because Jesus already died for our sins. The greatest blessing is to know God, and the Holy Spirit is making this happen right now: he is giving us a personal relationship with the triune God. It is as if he brings heaven right inside us. Heaven is where God is, and if we have the Holy Spirit, then God is with us wherever we go.

PROPERTY OF JESUS CHRIST

The Holy Spirit is the seal of our salvation, guaranteeing our inheritance. He is a deposit or down payment on eternity, backed by the full faith and credit of Almighty God. There is one further thing that the Holy Spirit does for every Christian, and that is to prove that we belong to God. This promise comes near the end

---

[13]Charles Hodge, *Commentary on the Epistle to the Ephesians* (New York: Robert Carter & Brothers, 1878), 64.

of verse 14, where Paul talks about the redemption of those who are God's possession.

The idea of possession may still be connected to the idea that the Holy Spirit is a seal. Seals had a number of functions in the ancient world. As we have seen, they were used to make a document secure and to indicate its authenticity. Seals were also used to prove ownership. When people put their seal on something, they were indicating that whatever they marked was their own personal property. Seals were used to show that something was someone's possession.

The Holy Spirit does the same thing for every believer in Jesus Christ. He is the seal that marks us as God's possession. If we have the Holy Spirit, it proves that we belong to God. Sometimes people wear "Property of" T-shirts: "Property of United States Air Force," "Property of Alcatraz Swim Team," and so forth. The Holy Spirit marks the Christian as "Property of Jesus Christ." This is part of the significance of Christian baptism, in which we are baptized in the triune name of the Father and of the Son and of the Holy Spirit. The sacrament of baptism is a visible sign that we belong to God. This is part of the sealing of the Spirit.

The Holy Spirit is the seal of our authenticity, the unmistakable sign that we belong to God. If the Holy Spirit is at work in our lives—if he is convicting us of sin, giving us faith in Jesus Christ, persuading us that the Bible is God's Word, enabling us to call God "Father," making us fruitful in ministry, and helping us to grow in grace—if the Spirit is doing any of these things at all, then no matter how much we are struggling in the Christian life, we have God's seal of our eternal salvation. The Bible says that God "has anointed us, and . . . has also put his seal on us and given us his Spirit in our hearts as a guarantee" (2 Cor. 1:21–22).

BLESSED ASSURANCE

What tremendous security this brings in all of life's difficulties! We may be disappointed or discouraged. We may be suffering from an unpleasant past, an unhappy present, or an uncertain future. Perhaps we doubt whether God even cares. Sometimes the difficulties are so great that we are tempted to despair.

But if we believe in Jesus Christ, then we are marked with his seal. God has fixed his Spirit on us. This seal will stay on us until our redemption, meaning our resurrection from the dead, the day when we finally receive the full benefit of the price that Jesus paid for our sins (cf. Eph. 4:30). The triune God has promised that he will bring us through all our troubles, into a joy that will never end. Do you believe this? Do you have the full assurance that comes from the sealing of God's Spirit?

The experience of one ordinary Christian family illustrates the importance of knowing the Holy Spirit and therefore having the assurance of eternal life. The family's patriarch was scheduled to have open-heart surgery. It was a triple bypass, back in the days when this was a relatively new procedure. His son and grandson drove four hours to visit him in the hospital. There the old man was, sitting on the edge of his bed, wearing his hospital gown, with his bare feet dangling a few inches off the floor. Then his son asked him how he was doing.

The man who needed surgery had been a Christian all his life. As an elder in the church, he had always believed in the plan of salvation from election right on to glory. Yet he said that the night before, as he lay alone in bed thinking about his life-threatening surgery, he had wrestled with God for the assurance of his salvation. "Is it really true?" he wondered. "I've said I believe it all these years, but will God really save me in the end?" He went on to testify to his family members that as he had cried and prayed and called out to God, he had received wonderful assurance of his salvation. He met God that night as he had never met him before, and by the morning he had complete confidence of his eternal security.

What gave the old man fresh assurance was the inward work of the Holy Spirit—the Spirit who was present in his baptism and drew him to faith in Christ, the Spirit who had sealed him until the day of his resurrection. By the gift of God's Spirit, this blessed assurance in the face of death is available to everyone who believes in Jesus Christ, according to the Father's plan.

This is all for God's glory. The whole plan of salvation magnifies the glory of the triune God, whose threefold work returns to his praise. The glory of God—this is the beginning as well as the end of our salvation.

In reading Ephesians 1 it is almost impossible not to be affected by its mood of joyful exuberance. In fact, the great Princeton theologian B.B. Warfield once remarked that Ephesians 1 should never be read in church: it should always be sung. This passage contains some of the most complex theological concepts in the entire Bible; yet the apostle Paul is not merely teaching, he is also praising God for the glory of his grace. In the Greek original, everything from verse 3 to verse 14 is one long sentence punctuated with praise: "*Blessed* be the God and Father of our Lord Jesus Christ . . . he chose us in him" (vv. 3–4); "In love he predestined us . . . to the *praise* of his glorious grace" (vv. 4–6); "In him . . . having been predestined . . . so that we . . . might be to the *praise* of his glory" (vv. 11–12); "In him you also, when you heard the word of truth . . . to the *praise* of his glory" (vv. 13–14).

This torrent of praise contains equal parts theology and doxology. The apostle wants us to do something more than believe the triune work of God in salvation—he wants us to experience the joy it brings to Christian life and worship. Whether we speak of the origination of salvation with the Father, the location of salvation in the Son, or the presentation of salvation by the Spirit, it is all to the glory of God.

2

THE MYSTERIOUS TRINITY

OUR TRIUNE GOD AND
HUMAN COMPREHENSION

Hear, O Israel: The LORD our God,
the LORD is one. (Deut. 6:4)

Beyond our utmost thought,
And reason's proudest flight,
We comprehend Him not,
Nor grasp the Infinite,
But worship in the Mystic Three
One God to all eternity. (Charles Wesley)[1]

The remarkable feature of Abraham's faith (in contrast to the surrounding religions of his day) was his devotion to *one* God. Standing along the border to the Promised Land, with polytheistic Mesopotamia behind him and polytheistic Canaan before him, Abraham defied both worlds by professing allegiance to *one* God as the *only* God. No other religion in the ancient world sustained such a bold, monotheistic claim.[2]

Three world religions—Judaism, Christianity, and Islam—stand in the heritage of Abraham's monotheism. But among these

---

[1]Hymn no. XLI, in *The Poetical Works of John and Charles Wesley: Reprinted from the Originals with the Last Corrections of the Authors; Together with the Poems of Charles Wesley Not Before Published*, ed. G. Osborn (London: Wesleyan-Methodist Conference Office, 1870), 7.338.

[2]Perhaps the closest parallel is Akhenaten's promotion of singular devotion to the Egyptian sun disk, Aten. Whether Akhenaten's reforms were actually monotheistic, and why they emerged and were thereafter reversed, remain a subject of scholarly debate.

three, Christianity stands apart: Christianity alone offers the further profession that this one, sole God is *triune* in nature. He is indeed *one God* (tri*une*), but he is *three Persons* (*tri*une)—Father, Son, and Holy Spirit.

As soon as this further, distinctive insight into God's nature is raised, questions swirl through the mind. How can it be that one God exists in three Persons? Is this view of God logical? Furthermore, is this New Testament view of God as Trinity theologically consistent with Abrahamic monotheism as taught in the Old Testament? These are not new questions but are questions the church has faced ever since the days of the apostles. In today's globalized, post-9/11 culture, it is becoming increasingly important for Christians to take seriously these logical and theological questions about the Trinity, particularly in the face of the rising influence of Islam. In this chapter we will explore these challenges and the church's historic answers to them.

Two questions are generally raised. First, there is the so-called *logical* question: How can 1 + 1 + 1 = 1? Second, there is the *theological* question: Is the New Testament doctrine of God's triune nature harmonious with the Old Testament doctrine of monotheism?

THE *LOGICAL* QUESTION

The first challenge usually raised in response to Trinitarianism is often presented as a logical question. How can 1 + 1 + 1 = 1? Is it even logical to conceive of one God in three Persons? Or is this claim a contradiction on its face, and thus an impossibility?

There is, indeed, a profound anomaly here. But it is just that—an anomaly, and no more. There is actually no problem with the logic of Trinitarianism. In reality, the difficulty that people sense and generally think of as a logical problem is actually an *analogical* problem.

If the church were saying that God is three *Gods* in one *God*, that would be a contradiction in logic. But the New Testament claim is that there are three *Persons* in one *God*. Think about this in mathematical terms. One can say that P + P + P = G (that is, three Persons constitute one God) and be completely logical. It is only if one were to claim that G + G + G = G (that three Gods are one God) that we should cry foul. However, the Church has always carefully maintained that all three Persons are fully divine because they share in one essential being. They are not three beings (three Gods) but one indivisible being (one God). This may be strange and mysterious, but there is nothing illogical about it.

When people begin to think about God's triune nature and say, "That doesn't seem logical," in reality it is not a contradiction in logic that they are sensing but something else. They are sensing the strangeness of the doctrine—there is something to this teaching about God that lacks *analogy* to anything else in human experience. It is unfamiliar to think of a being comprised of three Persons. While there may be nothing innately illogical about the idea, it is certainly unheard of in any other sphere of human experience and is thus strange to us. This is what we mean by saying that the so-called logical question is not really a *logical* question but an *analogical* question.[3]

A BEING WITHOUT ANALOGY

Typically, people come to understand the strange and unknown by drawing analogies to that which is already known and familiar. For example, when the first automobiles began to appear on the roads of early America, the expression *horseless carriage* was often used to identify them. This comparative expression helped introduce the public to a strange machine (the automobile) by comparing it to something already familiar (a horse-drawn carriage). Everyone knew what a carriage was, and this newfangled machine was

---

[3]Augustine observed (in *On the Trinity*, 5.9.10) that the doctrine of the Trinity is difficult because of the inadequacy of human language to explain it. Augustine's insight is another way of making the same point about the lack of analogy for this doctrine. Because human languages are formed around categories of human experience, the lack of human experience of trinitarian beings (other than God) leaves our languages devoid of terms to express it. Cf. V. Kärkkäinen, *The Trinity: Global Perspectives* (Louisville: Westminster John Knox, 2007), xiv–xvi.

simply a carriage that did not require a horse. Even if the inner mechanics of the automobile still befuddled the masses, its mystique was tempered by comparing it to something already familiar to people. This is how the human mind typically comes to understand (and to feel comfortable with) something unusual. But there simply is no analogy by which we can get comfortable with this anomalous being who is three Persons—not because his Three-in-Oneness is illogical, but because his nature is without comparison.

From the earliest centuries after Christ, many of the church fathers tried to find analogies that would alleviate this sense of strangeness. For instance, Gregory of Nyssa (c. 335–c. 400) liked to speak of a single current of water that, though being one water current, was made up of three parts: a ground-spring, its fountain, and its stream.[4] Ireland's St. Patrick (c. 387–493) is said to have used the three leaves of a shamrock when teaching the doctrine of the Trinity.[5] Waxing a bit more sophisticated, Augustine (354–430) spoke of love as a comparison to God's triune nature: one love exists only where there is one who is loved, one who loves, and the love itself.[6]

Interesting as these illustrations are, however, they all fall short of actually illustrating the triune nature of God. Some of these examples actually tend toward modalism—the mistaken view of God as one Person who takes on three different forms. The church fathers readily admitted the inadequacy of such examples. Augustine offered the careful disclaimer that his analogies were merely hints of the Trinity's likeness shadowed in creation, but wholly inadequate as actual comparisons.[7] Gregory Nazianzen (330–390) likewise admitted that the world provides no true analogies to help us understand this one being who is

---

[4]Gregory of Nyssa, *Ad Ablabium*, Cf. S. Coakley, "'Persons' in the 'Social' Doctrine of the Trinity," in *The Trinity: An Interdisciplinary Symposium on the Trinity*, ed. S. Davis et al (New York: Oxford University Press, 1999), 123–44.
[5]Alister E. McGrath, "The Doctrine of the Trinity: An Evangelical Reflection," in Timothy George, *God the Holy Trinity: Reflections on Christian Faith and Practice*, Beeson Divinity Studies (Grand Rapids, MI: Baker Academic, 2006), 17–35 (32).
[6]Augustine, *Trinity*, 8.10.14.
[7]Augustine, *City of God*, 11.28; *Trinity*, 9.2.2.

comprised of three Persons.[8] Nevertheless, modern thinkers and lay Christians continue to attempt analogies—such as C. S. Lewis's comparison between the three-in-one nature of God and the three dimensions of space[9] and the popular Sunday school analogies of the three states of water (ice, liquid, and gas) or the three parts of an apple (core, flesh, and skin).

In the end, the long history of such efforts to find analogies simply illustrates two points. First of all, there is no fully adequate analogy for the Trinity. With so many brilliant minds working on this effort over so many centuries, if some analogy did exist, it probably would have been identified and championed by now. But there is no true analogy to the Trinity. God's Trinitarian nature is an anomaly. Second, such a long history of efforts to find an analogy for the Trinity shows how pervasive this sense is among people of all times and cultures—the need for comparison to something familiar when trying to make sense of something mysterious. As long as there is no adequate comparison for God's three-in-oneness, the Trinitarian anomaly will retain its strange and mysterious character, and we will remain unable to comprehend it.

To summarize, the reason why God's triune nature boggles the mind is not because it poses a logical problem but because it poses an analogical problem. This is an important distinction to grasp, because something that is illogical is self-contradictory and cannot be true. But the fact that God's triune nature is strange and mysterious does not, in and of itself, rule against its truthfulness. Ironically, the unusual is a usual feature of life. Encountering anomalies is to be expected, especially when studying matters outside the realm of everyday experience.

THE NATURE OF ANOMALIES

Two of the great scientific advances of the twentieth century—the theories of relativity and quantum mechanics—illustrate the mind-

---

[8] Gregory Nazianzen, "On the Holy Spirit," Fifth Theological Oration, paragraph 33.
[9] C. S. Lewis, *Mere Christianity* (New York: Touchstone, 1996), 142–43.

boggling strangeness that sometimes characterizes the study of realms beyond everyday human experience.[10] Albert Einstein led the way into the discovery of relativity, with surprising insights into the relationship between our experience of time, space, motion, and gravitation. The seeming anomalies described by relativity theory are often associated with objects and movements at cosmic scales. Einstein also made important contributions to the study of physics at the atomic scale, uncovering some of the principles of quantum mechanics that describe bizarre happenings at the microscopic level. The emerging understanding of physics at both the macro and micro levels reveals truths about the universe that are anomalous compared to our everyday experience of the world.

In regard to the first of these theories (called "relativity"), astrophysicists tell us that time literally slows down for objects moving close to the speed of light, while time literally speeds up for objects moving more slowly. This bizarre phenomenon is often illustrated with the "twins paradox." In this thought experiment, one twin gets into a rocket ship traveling away from earth at 161,000 miles per second (86 percent of the speed of light), while the other twin remains on earth. When the twin on the rocket has been away for two and a half years, he turns around to make the return voyage at the same speed. He gets back to earth having spent approximately five years on his rocket ship. But he will return to find that his twin on earth has gone through roughly ten years of life during his absence. Though born on the same day, one twin would now have aged less than the other!

This is strange to us (and seems illogical) because in our everyday experience of time, time moves at a constant rate for everyone. However, physicists are careful to tell us that actually the rate of time's passage is not universal. A person who is stationary with a watch on his wrist while also watching a clock

---

[10]Thanks to Dr. Todd Pedlar, associate professor of physics at Luther College in Decorah, Iowa, for reviewing the physics examples in this section and providing helpful refinements.

that is moving past him would observe the moving clock's rate of time to be slower than the clock on his own wrist—if his perception were sharp enough to discern the slight variation. When people and clocks are moving at "normal speeds," the time dilation is slight enough that it is very hard to measure. It is only when we start to deal with movements approaching the speed of light that these changes in the way time passes are noticeable. In other words, there is a completely logical explanation for this scientific principle of relativity, but it will always be strange to us because we have no analogy to it in our everyday experience. One may be tempted to brush off relativity as untrue, but it is completely logical and has been repeatedly verified in scientific experiments. It simply remains strange for lack of a familiar analogy.

Similarly, quantum physicists tell us about strange realities on the microscopic scale of the universe. Subatomic *particles* of matter (for instance, electrons) sometimes act like *waves* in the world of the miniscule. They display what physicists call "wave-particle duality"—that is, they can display particle-like or wavelike properties depending on the experimental conditions to which they are subject. In the famous "double-slit" experiment, a series of electrons are fired one at a time from an electron gun through a screen with two parallel slits. Surprisingly, the electrons create a pattern characteristic not of particles passing through the slits, but a pattern exactly like that expected for waves passing through the slits. These particles behave as though they are waves! This would be like throwing baseballs through two windows onto a sandy shore and finding that the baseballs produced a pattern of many stripes in the sand rather than just two groups corresponding to the two windows. The characteristics of particles at the quantum level are completely different than expected by classical physics, and the wave-particle duality of electrons is just one small example of the strangeness of quantum mechanics.

As Niels Bohr (one of the fathers of quantum mechanics) famously said, "Any who says he understands quantum mechanics, doesn't know the first thing about it." Even the experts acknowledge the almost unbelievable oddities of what they observe in quantum physics. But this is because electrons operate in ways that have no apparent analogy in the interactions of the world of daily experience. One may be tempted to ignore such talk of quantum physicists as crazy, yet these strange phenomena are a real feature of nature.

Strangeness alone does not mean that something is illogical, much less that it is unreal. These two fields of modern physics, producing the doctrines of relativity and quantum mechanics, remind us that reality is full of strange phenomena. Such phenomena are difficult to come to grips with, not because they are untrue or illogical, but because they are unlike anything already familiar to us.

Like astrophysics and quantum physics, theology takes us into realms of reality beyond normal, this-worldly matters. When we study the very nature of God's being and make observations concerning *the kind* of being that he is, we should not be surprised at findings that are nothing like our experiences of other beings in the everyday encounters of our world. The discovery that God is triune is certainly one such finding. It is an anomaly, but it is not illogical. Nor is it to be dismissed as untrue because we cannot comprehend it. Rather, just as physicists examine the evidence of their fields to establish their doctrines about nature, the claim that God is triune has to be tested against what is revealed about him, and if the evidence sustains it, it must be accepted reverently. But unlike physics, which studies *material* phenomena, theologians study an immaterial God who cannot be examined through experiments with a telescope or a microscope. The only infallible evidence we possess for knowing God is his self-revelation in Scripture. It is, therefore, through the exegetical study of Scripture that the theologian must discern what is true about God, even if it stretches our mind beyond what we can fully comprehend.

So, here is the question before us: As God has revealed himself to his people through history as recorded in Scripture, do those encounters reveal God's nature as being triune or unitarian? Of course, as seen in the other chapters in this book, the New Testament presents the Trinitarian nature of God. But is the New Testament vision of the triune God consistent with the Old Testament evidence of God's nature, or is it (as Judaism and Islam charge) a violation of Abrahamic monotheism? This is the *theological* question that the Christian doctrine of God's triune nature must answer.

THE THEOLOGICAL QUESTION

After considering the so-called logical question facing Trinitarianism (which is really an analogical question), the Christian often faces the theological question—whether New Testament Trinitarianism is consistent with Old Testament monotheism. Through the centuries, the church has answered this question with a resounding yes. The Old Testament texts do reveal that the prophets of Israel recognized the inner-plurality of the one God of Israel, although the clarity of God's triunity was not fully grasped until New Testament times.

THE NATURE OF GOD'S REVELATION

Before we explore the Old Testament evidences for God's Trinitarian nature, our expectations need to be clarified. We need to be sure that we are realistic about what we *should* find in the Old Testament. On the one hand, Christians who want to "prove" the doctrine of the Trinity are sometimes tempted to demand too much evidence for this doctrine from the Old Testament Scriptures. On the other hand, those who want to "disprove" the doctrine of the Trinity are sometimes tempted to undervalue the evidence that is actually present and indeed pervasive throughout the Old Testament Scriptures.

Christians have sometimes tried too hard to show clear claims of God's three-in-oneness in the Old Testament Scriptures. For instance, medieval apologists have sometimes pointed to the story in Genesis 18 (three heavenly figures appeared to Abraham) as an Old Testament manifestation of the Trinity.[11] The passage begins, "And the LORD appeared to him by the oaks of Mamre, as he sat at the door of his tent in the heat of the day. He lifted up his eyes and looked, and behold, three men were standing in front of him" (Gen. 18:1–2). A more sober examination of the text reveals, however, that it describes an appearance of the Lord and two angels, not an appearance of the three Persons of the Trinity.[12]

Others have suggested that the three lines of the Aaronic benediction in Numbers 6:24–26 are an Old Testament witness to God's Trinitarian nature, since it states the name of God three times with each mention attached to a different line of blessing: "The LORD bless you and keep you; the LORD make his face to shine upon you and be gracious to you; the LORD lift up his countenance upon you and give you peace." Others have suggested that the threefold declaration of God's holiness in Isaiah 6:3 is a pointer to God's triune nature: "Holy, holy, holy is the LORD of hosts. . . ."

Such efforts to find a precise example of Trinitarianism in Old Testament texts are forced and strain the text.[13] As a starting point, we should admit that there is no clear articulation of Trinitarianism in the Hebrew Scriptures comparable to what we find in the New Testament. Nonetheless, there is a pervasive

---

[11]See, e.g., the 1411 painting by Andrei Rublev, *The Old Testament Trinity*, in the Cathedral of the Trinity in Zagorsk, Russia, reproduced in Igor Grabar et al, *USSR: Early Russian Icons* (Paris: UNESCO, 1958), Plate 24.

[12]So, e.g., Justin Martyr, *Dialog with Trypho*, 56. (Compare Gen. 18:22 with 19:1.)

[13]Cf. Gerald L. Bray, "Out of the Box: The Christian Experience of God in Trinity," in Timothy George, ed., *God the Holy Trinity: Reflections on Christian Faith and Practice* (Grand Rapids, MI: Baker, 2006), 39; Kärkkäinen, *The Trinity*, 8–10.

witness to God's inner-plurality in the Old Testament. The precise outlines of God's inner-plurality were not fully understood until the incarnation of the Second Person and the sending of the Third Person (at Pentecost) made the nature of God's triunity more clear. Nevertheless, the Old Testament writers were not completely ignorant of God's inner-plurality.

It is the normal pattern of biblical revelation that our understanding of God's nature increases with his unfolding revelation of himself through history. For instance, God first revealed himself to Abraham as *El Shaddai*, "God Almighty" (Exod. 6:3), meaning that he is the possessor of all power. He is not one god among many, but the sole source of *all* might. Then, in the stunning lesson on Mount Moriah at the end of his life, Abraham came to know God further as *Yireh*, the One who foresees and provides (Gen. 22:1–14). God not only provided the lamb to take Isaac's place on Mount Moriah, but, as Abraham recognized, one day he would provide another Lamb on that holy mount (see esp. v. 14). Abraham's knowledge of God expanded with his experience of God. Several centuries later, after long oppression in Egypt, God further revealed himself to Moses as *Yahweh*, the relationally present and faithful one (Exod. 3:14–15)—a name by which the patriarchs had not known God but the generation of Moses would come to know him.[14] These examples serve to illustrate a basic principle of God's self-revelation: over time we as the people of God

---

[14]The name *Yahweh* is defined in Exod. 3:13–15 by the sound-alike phrase, "I am"/"I will be" (*'ehyeh*). Though Hellenistically influenced interpreters (including the LXX) have often read this as a philosophical statement of God's self-existence, its Hebraic meaning (as brought out by its use in Exod 3:13–15, 6:2–8, and throughout the Old Testament) is relational: *Yahweh* describes the God "who is" in the concrete sense of his presence, his activity, his relational faithfulness among his covenant people. While the patriarchs knew to call God by this name (cf. esp. Gen. 4:26), it was only through the exodus event that the people came to know (i.e., *experientially* know; *yādā*) God as one who is covenantally and relationally present with and faithful to his people. Abraham received the promises but never saw them fulfilled; in the exodus, Israel became a vast people and did experience God's bringing them into the land. The Israelites came to know God as *Yahweh* in a way Abraham and the others believed him to be but never (experientially) knew him. Cf. R. Abba, "The Divine Name Yahweh," *Journal of Biblical Literature* 80 (1961), 320–28; S. Glisson, "Exodus 6:3 in Pentateuchal Criticism," *Restoration Quarterly* 28.3 (1985–86), 135–43.

discover more about him so that our understanding of his nature grows as our experience of his work of redemption unfolds.

This is seen not only in God's names but also in his worship. The worship of the patriarchs was relatively simple, offering a pale manifestation of the divine likeness to the generations of Noah, Shem, Abraham, and so on. Only after the exodus, and the dramatic experience of God's redemption in that generation, did Israel's worship expand to represent a fuller picture of God's nature as manifested in tabernacle worship. Once again, in the days of David, God revealed more of his kingly glory by granting landed rest to his people. With this new experience of God as one who settles his people and rules over them in peace, Israel's worship underwent extensive new changes with the fixed temple and its liturgies. These Davidic innovations reflected a more glorious vision of God—but not a different God. With the progressive unfolding of God's work in history comes increasing insight into his nature.

As explained in the New Testament book of Hebrews, a further change in worship takes place now that we have seen Christ. In the coming of Christ, heaven itself was manifested among us in ways only foreshadowed by the tabernacle and temple. In the ascension of Christ, our High Priest intercedes in the real throne-room of God. Our experience of God has improved even further in Christ, calling for new forms in worship that focus our hearts on all that we now know of God in the coming of Christ.

In other words, the Bible records a story whose main character (God) is revealed to us as the story is told. Every new twist in the plot reveals new complexities of and new insights into the great Protagonist's character. We must be careful, therefore, not to expect the clear vision of his triune nature encountered in the New Testament (only after the incarnation and Pentecost) to be as clearly presented in the Old Testament. The vagueness with which God's inner-plurality is described in the Old Testament records is not a problem for Trinitarianism—so long as the evidence of his inner-plurality is really there. But is it? We must ask carefully and honestly whether there is, indeed, plurality within the monotheistic God of the Old Testament, even if that plurality is not clearly defined in Trinitarian terms.

OLD TESTAMENT EVIDENCE OF THE TRINITY

Since the days of the early church fathers, numerous references have been identified throughout the Old Testament that provide glimpses of plurality within Israel's one God. For instance, the Old Testament speaks frequently of "*the* angel of Yahweh," a title that is used with much greater reverence than other passages that simply speak about "*an* angel" or "angels" from God. The Hebrew word for *angel* can also be translated "messenger" or "representative," and the Old Testament prophets recognized one particular Angel or Messenger of Yahweh who was distinct from others. Here is what is said of his appearance to Moses in a burning bush:

> And the angel of the LORD appeared to him in a flame of fire out of the midst of a bush. . . . And Moses said, "I will turn aside to see this great sight, why the bush is not burned." When the LORD saw that he turned aside to see, God called to him out of the bush. . . . (Exod. 3:2–4)

According to Scripture, the Lord God sent his Messenger—the one called "the Messenger of Yahweh"—to appear to Moses in the form of a flame in a bush. Furthermore, the same passage also unashamedly identifies this Messenger as God. When Exodus refers to the voice that spoke to Moses from the bush, it describes it as "*God* call[ing] to him out of the bush." This is after telling us that it was the Messenger (or Angel) of Yahweh who was in the bush. Such a description of God sending his Messenger who is in some sense distinct from himself but in some sense identified with himself is striking. If this passage were a lone example, it might not be so significant, but other Old Testament passages repeat this same awareness of God's Messenger as both distinct from and the same as himself.

Another example of this "Messenger of Yahweh" appears in Exodus 23:20–23, where the Lord says to Moses,

> Behold, I send an angel before you to guard you on the way and to bring you to the place that I have prepared. Pay careful attention to him and obey his voice; do not rebel against him, for he will not pardon your transgression, for my name is in him. But if you carefully obey his voice and do all that I say, then I will be an enemy to your enemies and an adversary to your adversaries. . . . My angel goes before you. . . .

In this passage, God speaks about sending "my angel" to lead the people into the Promised Land. He says that this Messenger has the authority to pardon or not to pardon sin, and that rebellion against him is inexcusable because "my name is in him." Indeed, to "obey *his* voice," God says, is the same thing as "do[ing] all that *I* say." The expression "my name is in him" is especially noteworthy. In Hebrew, a person's name is treated as one and the same with his identity. John I. Durham explains, "This latter statement is virtually an assertion of equivalence: the 'messenger' = Yahweh."[15] The inspired writer of this passage is either dangerously close to blasphemy by identifying an angel with God, or he was pressing the limits of the Hebrew language to introduce the Messenger of Yahweh as both distinct from God and one with God.

Throughout the rest of the story of the exodus and the conquest of the Promised Land, the Old Testament sometimes says that God spoke to Moses, to Joshua, or to the judges. At other times the Scriptures more specifically tell us that God spoke to these leaders of Israel through this "Messenger of Yahweh." When Joshua met "the commander of the army of the LORD" on

---

[15] John I. Durham, *Exodus*, WBC 3 (Nashville: Word, 1987), 335.

the outskirts of Jericho, he bowed to worship and received the same instruction that the Angel of the Lord had given to Moses at the burning bush: "Take off your sandals from your feet, for the place where you are standing is holy" (Josh. 5:13–15). Elsewhere in Scripture, angels are careful to stop humans from treating them with the reverence reserved for God alone (e.g., Rev. 19:10). But this Messenger of Yahweh receives the same worship that God himself receives, including this call for Joshua to treat his presence as holy in the same manner as Moses did at the burning bush. Once again Scripture describes the Messenger of Yahweh as both distinct from God and yet identified with him.

After the death of Joshua, the people of Israel rebelled. True to what God had warned Moses back in Exodus 23, the book of Judges tells us:

> Now the angel of the LORD went up from Gilgal to Bochim. And he said, "I brought you up from Egypt and brought you into the land that I swore to give to your fathers. I said, 'I will never break my covenant with you, and you shall make no covenant with the inhabitants of this land; you shall break down their altars.' But you have not obeyed my voice. . . ." (Judg. 2:1–5)

The Messenger once again speaks of the divine covenant with Israel as being *his own* covenant with them. Other references to this Messenger of Yahweh, not only in the exodus story but throughout the Old Testament, are similar in character (e.g., Gen. 16:7–13; 31:10–13; Judg. 6:12–24; 13:1–25). The Old Testament prophets may not have understood God's specifically *Trinitarian* nature, but as these passages illustrate, they were clearly aware of plurality within the God who both *sends* his Messenger and *is* this Messenger. In fact, the teaching of the New Testament on God's triune nature leans on Old Testament references like these.

For example, the New Testament epistle of Jude points back to the Old Testament teachings on Yahweh's Messenger, saying,

"Now I want to remind you, although you once fully knew it, that *Jesus*, who saved a people out of the land of Egypt, afterward destroyed those who did not believe" (Jude 5).[16] Jude was not reading New Testament theology back into the Old Testament story of the exodus; he was pointing to what is already present and pervasive in the exodus story: God both sent and was himself present in his Messenger to save (and discipline) his people on the way out of Egypt. Jude now reveals that the Messenger of the Lord in the exodus story is Jesus, the Second Person of the triune God.

The Old Testament title "Messenger of Yahweh" is probably synonymous with another, similar title in the Old Testament: "the Word of Yahweh." This second title is also used for the divine Spokesman who appeared to Old Testament saints, both revealing God's will to them and receiving their worship as being God himself. For example, in Genesis 15 we read:

> After these things the word of the LORD came to Abram in a vision. . . . And he [the word of the LORD] brought him outside and said, "Look toward heaven, and number the stars, if you are able to number them." . . . And he [the word of the LORD] said to him, "I am the LORD who brought you out from Ur. . . ." (vv. 1–7)

The fact that the author of Genesis understood "the word of Yahweh" as not only *speaking* to Abram but also *leading him outside* to show him the stars of the heavens has led many to understand "word of Yahweh" as another title for the Messenger of Yahweh. "The word of Yahweh" who came to Abram and to other Old Testament prophets was not just a voice but a messenger. To be clear, not every use of the phrase "the word of Yahweh" is a reference to this Messenger. For instance, in Deuteronomy 5:5 the term refers to the instructions (the literal *words*) given by

---

[16]On the textual question behind Jude's use of the name "Jesus" in this verse, see Philipp F. Bartholomä, "Did Jesus Save the People out of Egypt? A Re-examination of a Textual Problem in Jude 5," *Novum Testamentum* 50 (2008), 143–58.

God, as Moses says: "I stood between the LORD and you at that time, to declare to you the word of the LORD. . . ." But other uses of the phrase refer to the bearer of God's words to men and may be describing the same one elsewhere called "the Messenger of Yahweh" (e.g., 1 Sam. 3:21; 15:10; 2 Sam. 7:4; etc.).

Evidently the apostle John recognized this connection. He started his biography of the earthly ministry of Jesus by saying, "In the beginning was the Word, and the Word was with God, and the Word was God" (John 1:1). John recognized in Jesus the appearance of the one whom the Old Testament prophets met repeatedly and called "the Word of God"—a Divine Messenger who was with God and also was God. What was new in John's day was the fact that this Word "became flesh and dwelt [that is, remained] among us" (John 1:14). Rather than coming and going as he had in the days of Abraham and Moses and the prophets, the divine Messenger had now taken on human flesh and remained among men. With this extended experience with Jesus, more clarity concerning the nature of God than ever before became possible for the New Testament apostles. No passage in the Old Testament provides the kind of clear statement of God's triune nature that we find in John 1, Jude 20–21, Matthew 28:18–19, or 2 Corinthians 13:14. Nevertheless, even before the events of the New Testament era, the Hebrew prophets recognized some idea of plurality within the one God.

From the earliest centuries after the apostles, the Church Fathers explored such evidences for the Trinity in the Old Testament. They called such Old Testament glimpses of the Trinity *vestigia trinitatis,* meaning "footprints" or "shadows" of God's triunity. The presence of such Old Testament evidence has been important to the church. Our conviction concerning the triune nature of God is not founded solely on New Testament texts, but it has been important that the New Testament texts resonate harmoniously with the witness of the Old Testament concerning God's nature. As one writer summarized, "Nothing is more evident in the Old Testament than the fundamental oneness of God. Yet . . . the Old Testament reveals the unity of God to us as a *differentiated* oneness."[17] This Old Testament witness is an important part of the Church's confident confession of faith in the triune nature of God.

INTERTESTAMENTAL STUDY OF OLD TESTAMENT EVIDENCE

One might wonder if the early church fathers were just "finding what they were looking for" in the Old Testament. Obviously, if we start with the New Testament teachings about the Trinity, it might be tempting to read into the Old Testament texts more than they really mean to say. It helps to affirm the church's findings when we note that observations about the "differentiated oneness" of the Old Testament God were being drawn by Jewish exegetes long before the New Testament period. Jewish exegetes had recognized biblical marks of plurality within the monotheistic God of Israel long before the New Testament era. They never produced any explanations approaching the clarity of New Testament Trinitarianism (how could they, prior to the incarnation?). Nevertheless, the expressions of God's inner-plurality were recognized as such by Jewish exegetes even before the New Testament era.

Take, for example, the declaration of the Creator on the sixth day: "Then God said, 'Let *us* make man in *our* image, after *our* likeness'" (Gen. 1:26). There were extensive efforts by interstate-mental-era Jewish scholars to explain (or sometimes explain away!) its meaning by Jewish scholars in the intertestamental period.

The writer of a second-century BC Jewish book called *Jubilees* included a lengthy quotation of the Genesis creation account. However, he dropped the portion where God used plural self-references. *Jubilees* states, "And after all this he created man, a

---

[17]Timothy George, "The Trinity and the Challenge of Islam," in Timothy George, ed., *God the Holy Trinity* (Grand Rapids, MI: Baker, 2006), 116 (emphasis added).

man and a woman he created them" (2:14). The writer of *Jubilees* was probably avoiding God's plural self-reference by skipping God's quotation when copying that part of the account. It seems that the writer of *Jubilees* recognized the awkwardness of the one God using a plural self-reference. This example also shows one way in which intertestamental scholars might deal with such evidences—simply to ignore (or delete!) them.

Other ancient Jewish writers were more willing to face and try to explain this plural self-reference by God. A Jewish philosopher in Egypt named Philo (20 BC–AD 50) devoted a paragraph in his book *On the Creation* to explain why the plural self-reference of God exists in Genesis 1:26. According to Philo (24.72–76), God alone created on the first through the fifth days. On the sixth day, however, God invited the participation of "assistants" for the creation of man. Since God only creates what is good, and it served his purposes for man to be formed with a mixed capacity for good and ill, God employed others in the singular act of making man. While proffering this suggestion, Philo admits his continuing puzzlement, concluding, "It is plain that the real cause . . . is known to God alone" (v. 72).

The Jerusalem Talmud also reports a long tradition of Jewish scholars wrestling with this text. Lacking any clear answer, however, the Talmudic conclusion is that because God is described in the singular in Genesis 1:27, verse 26 must also be read with a singular sense even though the plural is used (*y. Ber.* 9:1, VI, A-G).[18]

In addition to such efforts to understand the plural self-references in Genesis 1:26, intertestamental literature hints at efforts to understand God's inner-plurality within other Old Testament texts also. There are discussions of references in Scripture to "the Angel of Yahweh" and "the Word of Yahweh," and intertestamental scholars were particularly fascinated by texts that spoke of God's "Spirit," his "Law," his "Glory," and his "Wisdom" in

---

[18]Cf. Millard Erickson, *God in Three Persons: A Contemporary Interpretation of the Trinity* (Grand Rapids, MI: Baker, 1995), 168.

ways that seemed to describe both personified agent(s) coming from God *and* God himself acting among men.

The first/second century BC Jewish book called *Wisdom* rehearsed the history of God's Messenger leading the people of Israel out of Egypt. Apparently equating the Messenger of Yahweh and the Word of Yahweh, *Wisdom* uses the latter title for the personal being whom God sent to accomplish the exodus: "Your all-powerful Word leaped from heaven, from the royal throne, into the midst of the land that was doomed; a stern warrior, carrying a sharp sword of your authentic command, he stood and filled all things with death" (18:15–16). Elsewhere in its report of Israel's travel from Egypt into the Promised Land, it is said that "a holy people and blameless race, Wisdom delivered from a nation of oppressors . . . and led them through deep waters" (10:15–18; cf. 9:1–2). The book of *Wisdom* is written in poetry, so these personifications of the "Word" and "Wisdom" may be poetic personifications and nothing more. However, when we recognize the role of "the Messenger of Yahweh" in the biblical exodus account, it seems likely that *Wisdom*'s personified references to the "Word" and "Wisdom" in retelling the same events are more than poetic personifications. They may be further examples of intertestamental efforts to make sense of the one who is both sent by God *and* is the presence of God in the Old Testament Scriptures.

We find nothing in the intertestamental writings approaching the doctrine of the Trinity that we find in the New Testament. Nevertheless, intertestamental scholars certainly recognized that the Hebrew Scriptures include references to plurality within God's self-revelation. Even if some saw these as awkward texts to be explained away, others saw them as valuable texts to be explored. What these examples tell us is that the early church fathers were not straining Old Testament expressions to fit their preconceived idea of God's triune nature. Long before the incarnation, the New Testament, or the early church fathers, Jewish scholars were already exploring the glimpses of God's inner-plurality that we now know as *vestigia trinitatis* ("shadows of the Trinity").[19]

THE NEW TESTAMENT BUILDING ON
OLD TESTAMENT EVIDENCE

The apostle John was standing upon an inherently Hebraic understanding of God when he began his Gospel, "In the beginning was the Word, and the Word was with God, and the Word was God" (John 1:1).[20] John was joining with those before him who already recognized the Old Testament references to "the Word" or "the Messenger" of Yahweh as at once being sent by God *and* being God. Repeatedly the apostle John presents his Trinitarian theology in terms consistent with—though always more than—the Old Testament categories of divine plurality.

In John 8:56–59, for instance, John reports Jesus' claim to have met with Abraham face-to-face:

> "Your father Abraham rejoiced that he would see my day. He saw it and was glad." So the Jews said to him, "You are not yet fifty years old, and have you seen Abraham?" Jesus said to them, "Truly, truly, I say to you, before Abraham was, I am." So they picked up stones to throw at him, but Jesus hid himself and went out of the temple.

The initial reason the Jews were upset with Jesus in this text is because he seemed to be saying that he was present with Abraham two millennia earlier. This is why the Jews responded with the aghast words, in effect, "You're not even fifty years old! How can you make such an absurd claim to have met Abraham?"

[19]For further material on intertestamental handling of God's "differentiated oneness," see Arthur Wainwright, *The Trinity in the New Testament* (London: SPCK, 1962), 15–40; Gerald O'Collins, *The Tripersonal God: Understanding and Interpreting the Trinity* (Mahwah, NJ: Paulist Press, 1999), 11–34; Richard Bauckham, *God Crucified: Monotheism and Christology in the New Testament*, Didsbury Lectures Series, 1996 (Carlisle, Cumbria, UK: Paternoster, 1998), 1–22; Robert Letham, *The Holy Trinity* (Phillipsburg, NJ: P&R, 2005), 17–33; Kärkkäinen, *The Trinity*, 3–7.
[20]Cf. D. A. Carson, *The Gospel According to John* (Leicester: Apollos, 1991), 115–16.

Jesus' further reply does not deny but indeed affirms that he had been alive in Abraham's day—and eternally before that. In telling us this story, John may be alluding to the statements in Genesis about "the Word of Yahweh" speaking face-to-face with Abraham (e.g., Gen. 15:1; 18:1).

John 12:41 similarly points to the commission that Isaiah received from heaven and explains that Jesus was the Divine Person who revealed that commission (and his own glory) to the prophet.[21] Throughout his Gospel, John reports Jesus' distinction from God as one sent by the Father and his identity with God as one with the Father (e.g., 8:29; 10:30; 17:21). In his report of the Upper Room Discourse (John 13:1–17:26), John presents one of the most penetrating presentations of Trinitarian theology anywhere in the Scriptures. In the intimacy of his Last Supper with the disciples, Jesus explains the deep, intra-Trinitarian love that bonds Father, Son, and Holy Spirit in their coordinated labors to adopt fallen people into that divine communion.[22] In other words, John points back to the *vestigia trinitatis* of the Old Testament as the framework within which he introduces the Word who had now taken on flesh and revealed the communion of the Trinity more intimately than ever before shown to humanity.

There is much that is new in the way the New Testament reveals God's Trinitarian nature. But intertestamental Jews, the New Testament apostles, and the early church fathers all recognized the presence of "differentiated oneness" within the God of the Old Testament. The doctrine of the Trinity only comes to full clarity in the New Testament, but it is consistent with the nature of God revealed in the Old Testament.

Naturally, New Testament-era Jewish sects that denied that Jesus was the Christ also refuted the apostolic witness to God's triunity. Whatever openness there may have been among earlier generations of Jewish thinkers, willing to consider the presence

---

[21]Cf. D. A. Carson, *The Gospel According to John*, 449–450.

[22]On Jesus' teaching about the Trinity in the Upper Room Discourse, see chapter 3 in this book.

of plurality within the one God of Israel, such openness collapsed in the face of Christianity. Rather like the case of the Apple iPhone devotee who sees no ill in the iPhone and finds no good in Google's Droid, open-minded study of Old Testament evidence on Yahweh's inner-plurality becomes extremely difficult now that the validity of entire religious traditions are determined by the outcome.

Unlike those intertestamental Jewish scholars who explored plurality within the oneness of God as revealed in the Old Testament writings, post-New Testament Judaism interprets Old Testament monotheism as inherently opposed to any "differentiated oneness" within God. While the Christian church has latched on to the *vestigia trinitatis* as real features of the Old Testament that cannot be ignored, post-New Testament Judaism has clung to the preponderance of monotheistic assertions in the Old Testament as grounds for minimizing or ignoring God's inner-plurality. But does this extensive emphasis on God's oneness in the Hebrew Scriptures really neutralize the validity of the *vestigia trinitatis*? Thus far we have considered some of the examples of "differentiated oneness" in the Old Testament. Does the extensive emphasis on God's oneness in the Hebrew prophets contradict such hints at God's inner-plurality?

RESPONDING TO THE EVIDENCE: CHRISTIANITY, JUDAISM, AND ISLAM

Monotheism is a prominent confession throughout the Bible. The purpose of the Old Testament confessions of monotheism is to assert the deity of one divine being, but it is not the purpose of these creeds to provide a "psychoanalysis" of that one God's inner being. Israel was surrounded by nations that believed that many warring deities governed the events of human history. According to polytheistic nations, what happened in history was the result of competing agendas among the gods. It was in opposition to the polytheism of the rest of the ancient world that Israel asserted its faith in one mind who governed over *all* the forces of the nations and over the whole of nature according to his sovereign will.

For example, in the biblical record of the flood, both the destruction of mankind in the flood and the saving of mankind in Noah's deliverance are regarded as the acts of one, single mind—the will of Yahweh (Gen. 6–9). The Babylonians had their own version of the flood account in which a very different picture emerges. In the Babylonian flood story, a council of angry gods agree to bring a flood to destroy mankind, but one god intervenes to save his friend Atrahasis (the Babylonian Noah). According to this polytheistic view of the world, one god (or council of gods) set upon an agenda to destroy, and some other god must be responsible for the agenda to save. This illustrates the popular conception of the ancient world, that many gods controlled the many powers of nature and of nations. This is a commonsense way to interpret the seeming ups and downs of history. The Hebrew faith seems counterintuitive in its bold conviction that all events—even simultaneous acts of destruction and salvation— came from one, sovereign throne. Yet that is the radical claim of monotheism.

Christianity, Judaism, and Islam all recognize monotheism as teaching this sovereignty of one God behind all events. Judaism and Islam, however, take the extra step of seeing in monotheism a "psychoanalysis" of God's inner nature. Christianity does not find this further deduction compelling.

Take, for instance, the Great *Shema*—undoubtedly the most important monotheistic creed of the Old Testament Scriptures: "Hear, O Israel: The LORD our God, the LORD is one" (Deut. 6:4). Moses first led the nation in reciting this great creed as they stood on the edge of the Promised Land. The New Testament apostles readily share this creed. In fact, Paul even quotes the monotheistic *Shema* as a *Trinitarian* creed in his letter to the Corinthians:

. . . "there is no God but one." For although there may be [among the idol-worshippers] so-called gods in heaven or on earth—as indeed there are many "gods" and many "lords" [among them]—yet for us there is one God, the Father, from whom are all things and for whom we exist, and one Lord, Jesus Christ, through whom are all things and through whom we exist. (1 Cor. 8:4–6)

Paul is quoting from the *Shema* in this passage, and he readily asserts that both Father *and* Son are the "one God . . . one Lord" of the *Shema*. (Elsewhere Paul makes similar claims regarding the Holy Spirit's participation in the Godhead.) For Christianity, the Triune God—Father, Son, and Holy Spirit—*is* the one God of the Great *Shema*. Paul understood this monotheistic creed not as a description of the inner nature of God's being, but as a bold confession that there is only one focus of worship, in contrast to the many competing foci of worship in pagan polytheism.

In Corinth (the community to which Paul addressed his exposition of the *Shema*) there were many temples to many different deities (the "many 'gods' and many 'lords'" he mentions). If a person were ill, he could seek assistance at the temple of Asklepios. If one were about to send merchandise to foreign ports, he could make offerings at the temple of Poseidon. Similarly, the temples of Apollo, Hermes, and other deities were to be attended according to their various realms of power. These temples did not represent competing religions, but the religion of Corinth ascribed the various powers of the created order to different deities. To be devout in Corinth, a person had to pay homage to all the right deities and be careful not to offend any of them. He had to love many different gods.

This was the standard view of the ancient world in which Old Testament Israel emerged. Not only did different deities control different natural powers, but different geographical regions (i.e., nations) were regarded as under different gods. If two nations went to war, the resulting victory was perceived as indicating a shift in authority among the gods in their contests with one another. Israel's monotheistic claim was radically different. In Israel's faith, there is only one God who is sovereign over all nations and their affairs. If Israel is victorious in battle against Assyria, it is because the God of Israel has given his people victory (e.g., 2 Kings 19:20). If the reverse occurs and Assyria is victorious in battle against Israel, it is because the God of Israel had given Assyria success and was turning over his people for discipline (e.g., 1 Chron. 5:26). In either case, it is one God who is sovereignly governing the outcome. Similarly, if a Hebrew needed to cry out for healing, for offspring, for agricultural produce, for a successful business venture, or for any other need, rather than going to the various high places and cultic sites of numerous deities, the devout Hebrew had one God to seek in all these matters.

The point of monotheism is that all the earth is under one divine throne, and all the powers of life and nature are under one God. Rather than juggling devotion to many different deities, as was common in the ancient Near East and in New Testament cities like Corinth, monotheism taught the sons of Abraham to love one God and to trust him wholly in all matters. At times Old Testament Israel faced the temptation to abandon Yahweh; but more often the prophets preached against the temptation to adopt other gods *alongside* their worship of Yahweh (e.g., 1 Kings 11:1–4). It was to guard against such divided loyalties that the doctrine of monotheism was repeatedly asserted by Moses and the ancient Hebrew prophets. But nowhere in the Old Testament does a monotheistic claim appear as an argument for peering into the nature of God's essence. The purpose of monotheistic claims is more practical: to keep Israel from adopting other pagan deities instead of—or alongside of—their worship of the one true God. Old Testament monotheism is not a psychoanalysis of God's inner being.

We see this meaning of monotheism (that it is a confession of God's sole sovereignty, not his "inner psychology") in Paul's exposition of the Great *Shema* to the Corinthians. But we see the same lesson in the context of the *Shema* itself, where Moses declares,

> Hear, O Israel: The LORD our God, the LORD is one. You shall love the LORD your God with all your heart and with all your soul and with all your might. . . . And when the LORD your God brings you into the land that he swore to your fathers . . . take care lest you forget the LORD. . . . You shall not go after other gods, the gods of the peoples who are around you—for the LORD your God in your midst is a jealous God. . . . (Deut. 6:4–15)

Deuteronomy gives us both the faith-claim of the *Shema* and its application. The application of monotheism given by Moses has nothing to say about God's inner nature but has everything to do with sole allegiance to him and to him alone. Judaism goes a step further when rabbis perceive in this monotheistic claim information about God's inner nature.

For instance, in the second of his thirteen principles of Judaism, the medieval Jewish scholar Maimonides elaborated on the *Shema* in this way:

> He who is the cause of everything is One, not like the unity of a genus and not like the unity of a species; and not like an individual entity which is a compound that can be divided into many unities; and not a unity like the ordinary body which is one in number but can be infinitely subdivided and partitioned. Rather, He, may He be exalted, is One and His unity is such that there is no other unity like it in any manner. This . . . fundamental principle is alluded to in the scriptural verse: *Hear, O Israel, the Lord, our God, the Lord is One.*[23]

---

[23]*Maimonides' Commentary on the Mishnah: Tractate Sanhedrin*, trans. Fred Rosner (New York: Sepher Hermon Press, 1981), 151.

Maimonides' intent in this statement was to rule out the various Trinitarian explanations he encountered, asserting that the *Shema* means God is unitarian in nature. As argued above, this claim introduces a meaning into the *Shema* beyond what its context supports. Christians (like Paul) confess with the *Shema* that there is only one God who alone rules over all while also accepting the witness of the Old Testament prophets to inner-plurality within that one God.

The centerpiece of Islamic confession is similar to the Jewish claim on this point. The fundamental confession of faith for Muslims is the assertion, "I bear witness that there is no god but Allah, and Mohammed is his prophet." This Islamic confession is further explained in the *Qu'ran*, where it is written, "They disbelieve who say: Allah is one of three (in a Trinity): for there is no God except One God." (5:73; cf. 4:171).[24] But this further conclusion—that God is solitary in his inner being—is not part of the monotheistic creeds of the Old Testament. Consistently, the monotheistic claims of the Hebrew prophets are given to assert divine sovereignty, not to provide divine "psychoanalysis" (cf. Exod. 20:3; Deut. 32:39; Psa. 72:18–19; Isa. 45:5–7).

As already shown, the Old Testament prophets actually found it possible to assert the *oneness* of Yahweh—his embodying all rule in one being—alongside their realizations that Yahweh exhibits a *plural inner nature* (e.g., sending his Word *and* being the Word). There is no contradiction between the Old Testament's claims to monotheism and the Old Testament's witness to God's inner-plurality. Instead the presence of both claims is an indication that the New Testament doctrine of God's triune nature opens up a great mystery already glimpsed by the Old Testament prophets.

---

[24]For further discussion of the Islamic polemic against Trinitarianism, see D. Thomas, ed., *Anti-Christian Polemic in Early Islam: Abū 'Īsā al-Warrāq's "Against the Trinity"* (Cambridge: Cambridge University Press, 1992).

RESPONDING TO GOD'S TRIUNITY

It is a basic tenet of orthodox Christianity that the whole Bible—Old and New Testament—reveals one, consistent plan of redemption carried out by one, unchanging God. But that does not mean that our understanding of God remains unchanged. From the beginning to the end of the Old Testament period, and through the New Testament era as well, there is increasing light and clarity as the revelation of God unfolds. In this chapter we have looked specifically at how the revelation of God's triune nature opens to us in the flow of Scripture.

But God's triune nature will always remain mysterious. It is not the intention of this chapter to explain God's triunity. In fact, it is commonly said that everyone in history who tried to *explain* the Trinity ended up being branded a heretic. Scripture does not present this doctrine in a manner that satisfies our curiosity. Instead it teaches us just enough about God's triune nature to increase our astonishment and awe of him. The point of this chapter has been to show that there is nothing illogical or theologically inconsistent about God's being three in one.

Having come to that conclusion, the mystery remains. But now, instead of a mystery that causes us to doubt, we see that God's triunity is a mystery that leads us to worship. Augustine wisely reminds us, "What is needed is a loving confession of ignorance rather than a rash profession of knowledge. To reach a little toward God with the mind is a great blessedness; yet to understand is wholly impossible."[25] In this chapter we have "reached a little toward God with the mind." But the purpose of such an exercise is not to satisfy questions; rather it is to clear away distractions and promote awe and worship.

As a God who demands holiness and then personally and graciously provides for sinners to be made holy, the *ways* of God stretch our comprehension. As a mighty Creator whose voice gave existence to all things, the *power and wisdom* of God

---

[25]Augustine, *Sermon 117*, translation from O'Collins, *The Tri-Personal God*, 11.

exceed our understanding. As one who exists eternally without beginning or end, never tiring and never changing, and who is everywhere present, with intimate understanding of all things, the *infinite* character of God is beyond our capacity to fathom. It certainly should be no surprise to us that when we undertake to contemplate the *very being* of so mind-boggling a God, we find ourselves facing a task to which our feeble minds are not equal.

The proper outlet for such awe is worship. True theology leads to doxology. Our task in this chapter is not complete without a call to worship. Intellectual contemplation of God is part of our calling to love him "with all our minds." But this exercise must be joined to loving God "with all our heart . . . soul . . . and . . . strength" as well (Mark 12:29–30).

Let us bow in reverence and awe before so profound and glorious a God—Father, Son, and Holy Spirit!

> Holy Father, Holy Son,
> Holy Spirit, Three we name you;
> While in essence only One,
> Undivided God we claim you,
> And adoring bend the knee,
> While we sing this mystery.[26]

---

[26]"Holy God, We Praise Your Name," based on *Te Deum* (fourth century). Attributed to Ignace Franz, c. 1774; translated by Clarence A. Walworth, 1853.

3

THE PRACTICAL TRINITY

OUR TRIUNE GOD AND THE CHRISTIAN LIFE

*The grace of our Lord Jesus Christ and the love of God
and the fellowship of the Holy Spirit be with you all.
(2 Cor. 13:14)*

*Father most holy, merciful and loving,
Jesu, Redeemer, ever to be worshipp'd,
Life-giving Spirit, Comforter most gracious,
God everlasting. (anonymous, tenth century)*[1]

Weddings are wonderful occasions. All the flowers and careful decoration of the room help make a wedding beautiful. The procession of the bride in her flowing gown, accompanied by her attendants, adds to a wedding's glory. The groom's expectant position at the front, dressed in his best and surrounded by his friends, lends nobility. And the exchange of vows at the climax of the ceremony gives a wedding a sense of solemnity and love.

Yet the greatest glory of a wedding is not in the ceremony itself but in the marriage that comes out of it. In the midst of a toy-strewn living room, with diapers to change and leaky faucets to repair, under the pressure of bills to be paid and jobs to fulfill, the true glory of marital love emerges. The reality of marital love

---

[1]From the tenth-century Latin hymn *O Pater, Sancte.* English translation from *Hymns Ancient and Modern: For Use in the Services of the Church with Accompanying Tunes* (London: William Clowes and Sons, 1904), #189.

is seen when the exalted images of the wedding ceremony are walked out in everyday life.

The believer's relationship with the triune God similarly calls for application in everyday life. The wonders of God's triune nature are not taught in Scripture simply for ivory-tower discussions. Scripture teaches us about God's triunity so that we might know him and relate to him more fully in our everyday lives. Contrary to common assumptions, the doctrine of the Trinity is not an impractical doctrine but needs to become a practical guide to our daily relationship with God.

Sadly, many Christians today rarely think of God's triune nature as a practical matter. As one theologian recently observed, "Despite their orthodox confession of the Trinity, Christians are, in their practical life, almost mere 'monotheists.'"[2] Of course, Christians *are* monotheists, believing that there is one God. Nevertheless, we often live as though we are *mere* monotheists whose God is One, but not three in one. Why is this?

Perhaps it is because this doctrine is so mysterious. Maybe many Christians assume that a doctrine as lofty as that of the Trinity cannot have much practical value. If so, this is an unfortunate mistake. Mystery is a healthy part of many relationships. Many married couples, for instance, spend their entire married lives striving to better understand the mysteries of the opposite sex. The preponderance of marriage books on the market—like John Gray's well-known *Men Are from Mars, Women Are from Venus*—remind us that mystery is a normal and healthy part of marriage. And if a growing understanding of one's spouse has practical implications for how a couple relates to one another, certainly the lifelong effort to know the mysterious Three-in-One should have practical implications for the Christian's daily relationship with him.

The practicality of the Trinity is especially clear in Jesus' Upper Room Discourse in John 13–17. After eating the Last

[2]Karl Rahner, *The Trinity*, trans. J. Donceel (New York: Crossroad, 1997), 10.

Supper with his disciples, Jesus began to speak to them about his imminent departure. The disciples were deeply troubled at Jesus' words about leaving them. In their thinking, for Jesus to leave them would bring a devastating break in their relationship with God. But Jesus spoke tenderly to his followers, giving them guidance for continuing (and even improving!) their walk with God after his departure. In giving this instruction for building their relationship with God, Jesus spoke extensively about God's Trinitarian nature. This passage of Scripture teaches us that the doctrine of the Trinity is practical and that knowing God as three in one should be at the center of our daily relationship with him.

While there is helpful instruction on the Trinity throughout Scripture, Jesus' Upper Room Discourse is a good place to focus. In this chapter we will look at each of the three Persons of the Godhead, one by one, as Jesus talks about them throughout the passage. In particular, we will seek to learn about the specific ways Jesus instructs us to respond to each of the three Persons in our daily Christian lives.

THE LOVE OF THE FATHER

The First Person of the Godhead is mentioned no less than sixty-three times in Jesus' Upper Room Discourse. Jesus uses three different titles for him in that teaching, the most prominent being the name "Father" (used fifty-two times). Jesus also calls him "God" (ten times), and once Jesus uses the metaphor "vinedresser" to describe him (in his parable about the Vine and the branches in 15:1–11). Each of these designations remind us that the Father is the *source* of all the Godhead's good purposes for us. In his discourse, Jesus mentions many examples of the Father's activities as the source of divine love, such as the following:

- *The Father sent the Son*: "The word that you hear is not mine but the Father's who sent me" (14:24).

- *The Father gave all authority to Jesus*: "Jesus, knowing that the Father had given all things into his hands . . . " (13:3).
- *The Father chose the ones whom he gave to Jesus to save*: "You [the Father] have given him [the Son] authority over all flesh, to give eternal life to all whom you have given him" (17:2).
- *The Father answers prayers*: "Whatever you ask the Father in my name, he [will] give it to you" (15:16).
- *The Father sends the Holy Spirit*: "And I will ask the Father, and he will give you another Helper, to be with you forever" (14:16).
- *The Father gives Jesus the word to teach us*: ". . . the word that you hear is not mine but the Father's who sent me . . . all that I have heard from my Father I have made known to you" (14:24; 15:15).
- *The Father is the source of love in the Godhead*: "The Father himself loves you, because you have loved me and have believed that I came from God" (16:27).

The First Person is commonly called "Father" because he is the initiator and source of heaven's love. In biblical times, a father was seen as the source of life in a family (as the begetter) and also as the source of provision and leadership to sustain and give identity to the family. Unfortunately, Christians sometimes miss this point. Some Christians mistakenly imagine that the name "Father" refers to some kind of "inner biology" within the Godhead. There may be clues to the Trinity's inner-connectedness in such titles; but if so, that is not their primary purpose. Scripture does not use Father/Son language for the first two Persons of the Godhead to teach us divine genetics.[3] "Father" is the preeminent title for the First Person primarily because it teaches us that he is the source of all the Trinity's purposes.

Jesus once explained the Father's role within the Godhead to a Jewish ruler named Nicodemus, saying, "God so loved the world, that he gave his only Son . . . " (John 3:16). Jesus wants us

---

[3]Cf. John Calvin, *Institutes*, 1.13.29.

to see God the Father as the source of the love behind the Son's work for our redemption (cf. John 10:14–18). We are accustomed to thinking of Jesus as the one who showed great love for us by his sacrifice on the cross, and we are right to marvel at Jesus' love. But it was not ultimately Jesus' love for us that sent him to the cross. It was the Father, primarily, who so loved the world that he sent the Son. This observation does not diminish the greatness of Christ's own love for us, for he shares the Father's love for the church (Eph. 5:2). Nevertheless, it is wrong to think of the Father God as being unloving (or indifferent) toward us until Jesus stepped in to do something about it (thus thinking of Jesus as the source of love within the Godhead). In his Upper Room Discourse, Jesus wants his disciples to recognize that it is *the Father* who is the source of all the love they have experienced from Jesus (cf. Rom. 5:8; Eph. 2:4; 1 John 3:1).

In human families today, many fathers are either absent dads or are present but uninvolved in their children's lives. Based on our cultural experience of fatherhood, we are apt to misinterpret the heavenly Father as also being a distant Person who rarely has time for us. This, Jesus urges us to understand, is not true. He is the source of all the Godhead's good purposes for his family.

That the Father is the source of the Godhead's love is not to deny that he also bears just wrath toward sin. The Father is also the source of all the Godhead's purposes in judgment. But the marvel of the gospel is that, in great mercy, the same Father who is grieved by human sin has himself initiated the work of divine mercy toward sinners. The Scottish theologian William Symington explained, "The true view of the matter is this, [the Father's] divine love is the cause of the [Son's] atonement, and not that [the Son's] atonement is the cause of [the Father's] divine love. . . . The gift of His Son is ever regarded as the most perfect manifestation of

God's grace."[4] John Owen uses the analogy of a flowing fountain and the radiant sun when he affirms, "Jesus Christ, in respect of the love of the Father, is but the beam, the stream, wherein though actually all our light, our refreshment lies, yet by him we are led to the fountain, the sun of eternal love itself. Would believers exercise themselves herein, they would find it a matter of no small *spiritual* improvement in their walking with God."[5]

RESPONDING TO THE FATHER'S LOVE

The first and most important implication of Jesus' lessons on the Father, then, is that *we would come to know him as the fountain of divine love.* As we do so, we will learn to recognize him as the source of the encouragement we receive in the Scriptures, in answers to our prayers, in the grace of the Holy Spirit in our lives, and in all the other blessings we receive. Jesus teaches us to thank the First Person of the Godhead—the Father—as the One who sends all these blessings to us.

Once we begin to think rightly about the heavenly Father, a series of additional, practical responses follow. Because the Father is the *source* of all, Jesus teaches us that he is also to be served as the *object* of all. He is the One to whom we respond with love, with prayers, with worship and adoration. We also worship the Son and the Holy Spirit, but because even the Son and the Spirit give glory to the Father and share in his glory (e.g., John 16:14–15; 17:4–5), we worship the Three-in-One with an understanding that the Father, the source of all, is the ultimate object of all. This means that *we should address our prayers especially to the Father*, both in thanksgiving for blessings received and in petition for our needs.

Jesus taught his disciples to pray to the Father, saying, "In

---

[4] William Symington, *On the Atonement and Intercession of Jesus Christ* (New York: Robert Carter & Brothers, 1863; reprint, Grand Rapids: Reformation Heritage Books, 2006), 21–22.

[5] John Owen, *Of Communion with God the Father, Son, and Holy Ghost*, ed. William H. Goold, in *The Works of John Owen*, Vol. 2 (Edinburgh: Banner of Truth Trust, 1980), 23 (italics in original).

that day [i.e., after Jesus' return to the Father] you will ask nothing of me. Truly, truly, I say to you, whatever you ask of the Father in my name, he will give it to you . . . you will ask in my name, and I do not say to you that I will ask the Father on your behalf; for the Father himself loves you . . . and now I am leaving the world and going to the Father" (16:23–28). Jesus is not ruling out the appropriateness of praying to the Son or to the Holy Spirit, but he is teaching us that the ultimate focus of Christian prayer is "Our Father in heaven" (cf. Matt. 6:9–13). The disciples were accustomed to telling Jesus about all their needs—and understandably so, for he was right there with them! But Jesus wanted his disciples to know that his departure would not weaken their access to help. Instead, because the Father is the ultimate source of answered prayer and Jesus was going to the Father, the disciples' prayer lives would actually be strengthened by his departure.

We can only approach the Father in the name of Jesus. Nonetheless, Jesus' intercession truly opens the way for us to address the Father in prayer. Jesus is not a middleman who insists on keeping the people and the provider apart. The typical retail store today illustrates the kind of middleman who hides sources to keep people buying through them so they can get a profit for themselves. But a true mediator brings people together, and Jesus is that kind of mediator. One of the practical implications of this is that the Father, as the source of all heaven's blessings, should also be the ultimate object of our prayers (offered in the name of Jesus and aided by the Spirit; cf. Rom. 8:26–27, 34). Because the three are one and equally God, the priority of prayer to the Father must not be pressed to the extreme of never praying to Jesus or the Holy Spirit. We have examples of prayer to other members of the Godhead in the Scripture (e.g., Acts 7:59–60). However, the prevailing pattern of prayer in the Bible is to address the Father in the name of the Son by the help of the Holy Spirit (e.g., Eph. 1:17; 3:14).

We also should honor the Father with the fruits of our lives.
Jesus included this further lesson in his discourse through a parable about a vine. "I am the true vine," he said, "and my Father is the vinedresser. Every branch in me that does not bear fruit he takes away, and every branch that does bear fruit he prunes, that it may bear more fruit. . . . I am the vine; you are the branches . . . apart from me you can do nothing" (15:1–5). Just as a vineyard owner plants his vines in order to receive a harvest, so the Father as the source of all (the Vinedresser) rightly receives the fruits that Jesus (the Vine) brings to our lives (the branches).

The Old Testament prophets frequently spoke of Israel as the vine of the Lord (e.g., Isa. 5:1–7), but the prophets also had to reprove Israel for failing to bring forth good fruit. This is why, in his conversation with his disciples, Jesus explains, "*I* am the *true* vine." Jesus is explaining that *he* is the one who fulfills the Vinedresser's purpose for Israel. The fruitful vine that Israel failed to be *without* Christ, we now become *in* Christ. Jesus tells us that we are the branches through whom he provides the fruits the Father desires. As we drink deeply from Jesus' words ("If you abide in me, and my words abide in you," 15:7) and pray accordingly ("ask whatever you wish . . . that you bear much fruit," 15:7–8), Jesus makes us fruitful and pleasing to the Father. "By this [i.e., abiding in the Word and prayer] my Father is glorified, that you bear much fruit and so prove to be my disciples" (15:8). In considering this parable, we are beginning to think about the Second Person of the Godhead and his vital role in our lives. But we also must note that it is the Father ("the Vinedresser") who is the ultimate recipient of the fruits that Jesus successfully brings into our lives.

We often succumb to the mistaken idea that "God's chief end is to glorify me and help me enjoy myself forever" and that Jesus' death was to pay for my sins so I can keep on enjoying my life without God getting on my case. In his Upper Room Discourse, Jesus gives us a vision of the First Person of the Trinity that challenges that error. It is a vision that leads us into a fruitful Christian life in relationship with a Father who loves us.

THE MEDIATION OF THE SON

The Second Person of the Godhead is named forty-three times in the Upper Room Discourse, and he is ascribed with seven different names and titles. He is called "Jesus" or "Jesus Christ" twenty-one times. The disciples recognize him as "Lord" or "Master" thirteen times. He refers to himself as our "Teacher" two times. He is called the "Son" (that is, the Son of God) several times explicitly (three times), and this relationship is inferred many more times in Jesus' references to God as "my Father." He is also called the "Son of Man" (once). Jesus identifies himself as "The way, and the truth, and the life" once, and he is called the "Vine" two times. All of these titles for the Second Person of the Godhead draw our attention to his *mediating* role and our relationship to him as our Mediator. As the Father is the source and object of all the Godhead's purposes, the Son is the one who mediates the Father's love to us and who mediates our prayers and fruit-bearing to the Father.

In the modern West, we often miss the biblical significance of the Father/Son titles ascribed to the First and Second Persons of the Godhead. In our culture, these titles are used only in family relationships. In other spheres of life, such as business or politics, we use different terms to describe people—terms like president, secretary, or business agent. In the biblical world, however, businesses typically *were* family affairs. The father was not only the head of the family, but he was also the head of the family business, whether it was a family farm, carpentry, a family medical practice, or something else. A father would train his sons, and they would work with him in the family trade. In fact, in the rare situation when a young man in ancient Israel left his family trade to learn another, the language of sonship was used to describe his new assignment. He would become the "son" of the one in whose home he now labored, as illustrated by the men who studied in Elisha's seminary and were called "the sons of the prophets" (e.g., 2 Kings 4:38). Likewise in politics: before ideas of periodically electing new leaders became widespread, government was largely a matter of families (dynasties). The title "sons of the king" brought to mind not only family relationships but political authority. Among all the court officials in a king's government, it would be his sons (and his heir, most of all) who exercised chief authority as the leader(s) of armies and other political initiatives.

In biblical language, then, the Second Person's name "Son" is full of profound implications. To use contemporary equivalents, he is the authorized business agent, the high prince, the commander of the troops, the authoritative spokesman, the overseeing architect, the CEO or COO, and so forth. He was responsible to implement the Father's vision. Here are some representative passages about the Son's work from the Upper Room Discourse:

- *Jesus reveals the Father to us*: "Jesus said to him, 'Have I been with you so long, and you still do not know me, Philip? Whoever has seen me has seen the Father'" (14:9).
- *We pray to the Father in Jesus' name*: "In that day you will ask nothing of me. Truly, truly, I say to you, whatever you ask of the Father in my name, he will give it to you" (16:23).
- *Jesus sends the Spirit from the Father to us*: "And I will ask the Father, and he will give you another Helper, to be with you forever" (14:16).
- *Jesus brings the Father's words to us*: ". . . the word that you hear is not mine but the Father's who sent me" (14:24).
- *Jesus brings us to the Father*: "I am the way, and the truth, and the life. No one comes to the Father except through me" (14:6).

Many religions claim to bring us divine truths. But any theology that ignores the revelation and work of Jesus Christ in its teachings about God is ultimately a false religion. As the Son, the

Second Person of the Godhead is the authoritative spokesman of heaven's will and the sole agent who brings people into right relationship with God.

During the Upper Room Discourse, the disciple Philip started to get Jesus' point about the Father's great love, but he misunderstood the role of Jesus as the revealer of that love. Philip said to Jesus, "'Lord, show us the Father, and it is enough for us.' Jesus said to him, 'Have I been with you so long, and you still do not know me, Philip? Whoever has seen me has seen the Father. . . . Do you not believe that I am in the Father and the Father is in me?'" (14:8–10). Everything that Jesus does *is* the Father's love being brought to us. Understanding that God the Father is the source of love does not mean that we somehow relate to the Father independently from our relationship with Christ. On the contrary, we can only know the Father through the mediation of the Son. In knowing Jesus, we are at the very same time learning to love the Father. Jesus Christ is the perfect representative of the Father to his people, and we cannot know the Father apart from him.

This mediation by the Son is not restricted to the thirty years or so of his earthly ministry. As we saw in chapter 2 of this book, long before he took on human flesh and lived among us, the one whom the Old Testament prophets knew as "the Messenger of Yahweh" was already at work mediating the Father's purposes to men. Jude wrote in his epistle about "Jesus, who saved a people out of the land of Egypt" (Jude 5). The apostle John tells us about Christ, saying, "In the beginning was the Word. . . . And the Word became flesh and dwelt among us" (John 1:1, 14). Although the Second Person of the Trinity was not called "Jesus" until he took on human flesh in the New Testament period (Matt. 1:21), he was the same Divine Person who had been implementing the Father's agenda of creation and redemption all through history.

In his Upper Room Discourse, Jesus was assuring his disciples that even though he was returning to heaven and would no longer dwell among them bodily, he nonetheless continues in his eternal role as the Son, and through the words he brought to us he will continue to mediate the Father's love to us. "I will not leave you as orphans," he said, "I will come to you. Yet a little while and the world will see me no more, but you will see me . . . he who loves me . . . I will love him and manifest myself to him" (14:18–21). In other words, Jesus continues to mediate the Father's love to people even after his ascension. One of the disciples expressed his confusion at how Jesus could be simultaneously gone from the world and continue to reveal himself to the disciples. He asked Jesus, "'Lord, how is it that you will manifest yourself to us, and not to the world?' Jesus answered him, 'If anyone loves me, he will keep my word, and my Father will love him, and we will come to him and make our home with him'" (14:22–23). Jesus continues to mediate the Father's purposes to the church through his Word. Jesus was the mediator of the Father's words to the Old Testament prophets and the mediator of the Father's words to the New Testament apostles, and he continues to be with his people in the Word.

RESPONDING TO THE SON'S MEDIATION

The most important response that we must make to the Son is to *look to him to bring us into favor with God*. There are many places we can turn to see glimpses of God's majesty and goodness. To a certain extent, every person can know things about God simply by examining the creation and its marvels (Rom. 1:20). Many religions and philosophies in the world discern noble and wise principles through insight into nature and human nature. Confucius had many profound insights into human society that continue to be revered. Aristotle, Plato, and the other classical Greek philosophers left penetrating analyses of nature and human society in their writings. Even pagan religions—like the complex superstitions of the ancient Egyptians or the pantheons of the Greeks and the Romans—were, as Paul put it, men "seek[ing] God, in the hope that they might feel their way toward him" based on his creation order (Acts 17:27).

But it is only in the words and work of the Second Person of the Godhead that the true likeness of the Father, and the reliable and authentic way of finding favor with him, is provided. "I am the way, and the truth, and the life," Jesus said, "No one comes to the Father except through me" (John 14:6). The most important practical implication to draw from our understanding of the Second Person's role in the Godhead is to trust in his work of atonement and intercession alone to find favor with God.

A second implication that Jesus teaches us is that *we should join ourselves with other believers—specifically as members of a local church*. Several times in his Upper Room Discourse, Jesus instructed his disciples about this: "A new commandment I give to you, that you love one another: just as I have loved you, you also are to love one another. By this all people will know that you are my disciples, if you have love for one another" (13:34–35; cf. 13:13–17; 15:12). Jesus is teaching us to worship and serve him together, and not as loners (15:9–17). When the apostles went out with the gospel and formed local congregations, they were not forming churches simply because it seemed like a good idea to them. They were obeying the instruction Jesus gave to them in his Upper Room Discourse. Jesus calls all of his disciples to respond to the love of the Father that the Son brings to us by loving one another in communities of disciples.

Jesus' role as Mediator also means that *we should pray to the Father in his name* (16:23). Most Christians add the phrase, "In Jesus' name, amen," at the end of their prayers. These are not magic words, like abracadabra, that mystically add more power to our prayers. When we pray in Jesus' name, we are acknowledging that Jesus is the one who did what was necessary to bring our prayers to the Father.

By way of analogy, consider a person who writes a letter and decides he does not like the stamps produced by the Post Office.

Instead he draws a little picture on the top corner of the envelope. Or maybe he finds a sticker to put there. Maybe he even uses a stamp from a foreign country that he likes better. In none of these instances will the letter get to the intended destination. Only the government-approved stamp will work, because it represents that the proper payment has been made to the proper authorities for the delivery of this letter.

In the same way, we should always pray in mindfulness of Jesus' death on the cross and his ascension to the presence of the Father where he now intercedes for us (Heb. 4:14–16). We must pray, in other words, in a spirit of repentance and faith in Christ's merits, not presuming to approach the Father in our own goodness. Whether or not we say the words "in Jesus' name" at the end of our prayers, praying in Jesus' name means praying with faith in what he has paid (his substitutionary death) to the proper authority (the Father) in order to make our prayers efficacious.

Finally, because Jesus is the one who brings the Father's words to us (14:24), we respond to his role within the Trinity by *using the Scriptures as the standard for our faith and life.* As we saw earlier in this chapter, Jude emphasized that it was *Jesus* who was "the Word of Yahweh" and "the Messenger of Yahweh" in Old Testament times, leading the people into their promised salvation. Jude emphasized this because in his day, "certain people have crept in unnoticed" into the church promoting new teachings by "relying on their dreams" and their own understanding of what God wants (Jude 4, 8, 10). Jude's exhortations are relevant for us today as well. Many today look and sound like Christian teachers, but their teachings arise from their own reasoning or even from dreams and visions, without grounding their teaching in the careful study of what Jesus, as the Divine Revealer of God's will, has provided for us in the Word. As we come to know the Second Person of the Godhead as the one who accomplishes the role of the Son, we ought to respond by subjecting every other teaching or philosophy to the ultimate instruction of Scripture.

We study the Scriptures in order to know the Father's purposes through the mediation of the Son.

God the Father is the source of heaven's love, but no one can know that love apart from the mediating work of the Son. It is only through Christ that people come to God and grow in him.

THE PRESENCE OF THE SPIRIT

Jesus had much to say about the Third Person of the Trinity in his Upper Room Discourse. The Spirit is only named eight times in this Discourse, but these identifications occur in five extended discussions (14:16–17; 14:25–26; 15:26–27; 16:7–11; 16:12–15), giving him a prominent place in this teaching of Jesus.

Three different names are used for the Spirit in the Upper Room Discourse. He is called "the Spirit of truth" (three times). He is called "the Holy Spirit" (once). And four times he is called "the Helper" (sometimes translated as "Comforter," "Counselor," or "Advocate"). Each of these titles for the Third Person of the Godhead is used by Jesus to emphasize his particular role as the one who takes God's love and truth as it has been revealed and accomplished in Christ and administers it to the particular needs, places, times, and circumstances of God's people.

The disciples were greatly saddened to think of Jesus' departure. Jesus' lessons on the *Father's* love as the source of all the Godhead's good purposes and his lessons about his own mediation as the *Son* who reveals and accomplishes all those purposes for us were designed to bring comfort and practical guidance to the disciples on the eve of his leaving them. But even with such glorious purposes appointed by the Father and accomplished by the Son, we still need God's nearness with us in the myriad circumstances of our individual lives. Therefore, Jesus also instructed his disciples on the role of the Third Person of the Trinity, the *Spirit* or *Helper*, as the perpetual minister of God's presence among us. Here are some representative statements:

- *The Spirit remains with us forever*: "I will ask the Father, and he will give you another Helper, to be with you forever, even the Spirit of truth . . . [who] dwells with you and will be in you" (14:16–17).
- *The Spirit reminds us of the Son's words from the Father*: "These things [the Father's words] I have spoken to you while I am still with you. But the Helper, the Holy Spirit . . . will teach you all things and bring to your remembrance all that I have said to you" (14:25–26; cf. 16:12–15).
- *The Spirit leads the church in witness*: "But when the Helper comes . . . he will bear witness about me. And you also will bear witness" (15:26–27; cf. 16:7–11).

In all history, there never was a more marvelous display of God's presence with his people than the incarnation. In the mystery of the incarnation, the Son of God took on a location-limited human nature along with his omnipresent divine nature. In his humanity Jesus located himself with twelve disciples. Those disciples had the marvelous privilege of experiencing God the Son's active presence among them, not only revealing the Father's will to them, but also applying it to their specific needs on a day-by-day basis. John wrote with awe, "We have seen his glory, glory as of the only Son from the Father, full of grace and truth" (John 1:14; cf. 1 John 1:1). Having the Son of God present with them gave the disciples peace in the face of opposition (e.g., John 6:66–69), courage to witness (e.g., Mark 6:7–13), understanding to dispel their confusion (e.g., Mark 4:10–11, 34), strength to hear rebukes and to grow by them (e.g., Matt. 16:23), humility to resolve conflicts with one another (e.g., Luke 22:24–27), and joy in the assurance of God's faithful love for them (e.g., Luke 22:31–32). Having the redemptive presence of God manifest in their midst was, for the disciples, an indescribable source of comfort and strength. We can understand how distraught they must have been when Jesus announced that the time had come for him to depart.

In the face of such sorrow, Jesus lifted the hearts of his disciples with a wonderful promise. Although he was departing to the Father, Jesus announced, "I will ask the Father, and he will give you another Helper, to be with you forever, even the Spirit of truth" (John 14:16–17). Note that Jesus describes the Spirit as "*another* Helper." The same kind of help that Jesus had provided to the disciples, the Spirit would now continue to provide. The disciples would not be left alone. Jesus' departure was not a removal of God's gracious presence from their midst. On the contrary, rather than twelve men, alone, knowing the "helping" presence of Christ in their midst, believers everywhere, through the Spirit, would have the powerful presence of God. "I tell you the truth," Jesus said, "it is to your advantage that I go away, for if I do not go away, the Helper will not come to you. But if I go, I will send him to you" (16:7).

As an analogy, think of a young college graduate starting a new job. Imagine he was hired as a sales representative for a big company. On his first day, he is given a job description that provides instructions for his new position: "Build and maintain customer relationships to meet and exceed sales goals," "Proactively communicate with clients to provide customer service and ensure repeat customers," and other similar instructions. These are clear instructions, but they are also generic. They are instructions designed to guide all of the company's sales reps in their various responsibilities. The young man is going to have to make decisions as he applies these instructions to his work with customers. He may end up with an angry client on the phone, complaining about a late shipment. As a sales rep, this young man will remember his responsibility to "build and maintain customer relationships" and will strive to come up with the right responses to resolve the problem on behalf of the company. As clear as the general instructions of his job might be, he still has to make specific applications of them on a daily basis.

In a similar way, the revelation of Christ in the Scriptures provides a rich and thorough description of God's grand purposes for his world and his holy will for each of us. The Scriptures also teach us what Jesus has done, and continues to do, to accomplish those purposes. But we still have to make day-by-day responses to God's will as we apply his truth to our various circumstances. Instructions like "love your neighbor" (Matt. 19:19) need to be applied to specific circumstances. When the disciples had Jesus with them bodily, he provided day-by-day, circumstance-by-circumstance guidance. With his departure, the disciples would lose that intimate presence of God in their midst—or so they feared. But Jesus comforted the disciples with the promise of "another Helper," one who would be with them forever. Indeed, the Spirit would not only be with this small circle of twelve, but he would be with all God's people to help them. The ministry of the church would expand in even greater joy and power when Jesus ascended to the Father and sent the Spirit. He said, "Truly, truly, I say to you, whoever believes in me will also do the works that I do; and greater works than these will he do, because I am going to the Father. . . . If you ask anything in my name, I will do it. . . . And I will ask the Father, and he will give you another Helper, to be with you forever" (John 14:12–16).

The book of Acts documents how the triune God did expand his redemptive work in the world after Jesus' ascension. The Father sent the Spirit at Pentecost (Acts 2:1–41), and Acts reports how the Spirit-empowered church carried on the work of Christ in Jerusalem (Acts 2:42–8:3), in Judea and Samaria (Acts 8:4–12:25), and to the uttermost parts of the earth (Acts 13:1–28:31). But the story of the book of Acts is not over. The book ends with a cliff-hanger: the last paragraph of Acts ends with Paul in prison in Rome, and the outcome of his witness is left unfinished. By ending with an unfinished story, Acts is telling us that the work continues. It is up to us, empowered by the same Holy Spirit, to continue the story.

RESPONDING TO THE SPIRIT'S PRESENCE

What are some of the practical implications of the Spirit's presence for our lives? First, because of the promise of the Spirit, *we should expect the Spirit to instruct our decisions through the Word*. This does not mean the Spirit will mystically produce new meanings from the Bible tailored to our individual questions. But it does mean that we should expect the Spirit to help us as we bring our lives under the light of God's Word.

A word of clarification should be made at this point in view of certain misunderstandings about the Spirit's work we sometimes encounter. Jesus makes it clear to us that he is the one who brings us all the Father's words. The Son is the revealer. "The Spirit of truth" would bring to the disciples' remembrance everything Jesus taught them (John 14:26) and would guide them in their further understanding of "the things that are to come" (16:12–15).[6] The Spirit applies the words and work of Jesus, but he is not the mediator of new words from the Father. Sometimes Christians confuse the roles of the Son (the agent of the Father's words) and the Spirit (our Helper in responding to the Word), resulting in too low a view of Scripture and an overemphasis on ecstatic experiences from the Spirit. It is evident in the book of Acts that even those who received supernatural guidance from the Spirit in the New Testament church were being led by those visions to a reverent response to the Word.

In the account of Pentecost, for example, when the Spirit fell in tongues of fire upon the 120 disciples, the purpose of this outpouring was to empower the disciples for their preaching of the Scriptures (Acts 2:1–36). Likewise, when a controversy arose about the inclusion of uncircumcised Gentiles in the church, Acts tells us that it was after James brought the Scriptures to bear on the situation (Acts 15:13–21) that the church leaders professed

---

[6]Note that "the things that are to come" probably referred to the cross and resurrection, which the Spirit would help the disciples to understand. Cf. D. A. Carson, *The Gospel According to John*, Pillar New Testament Commentary (Grand Rapids: Eerdmans, 1991), 539–42.

the Spirit's guidance in their conclusions (Acts 15:28). When we look at the New Testament epistles, we find that the Spirit was inspiring the writers as they studied the Old Testament Scriptures and the words of Jesus. This is what Jesus taught about the Spirit's role: "He will glorify me, for he will take what is mine and declare it to you. All that the Father has is mine; therefore I said that he will take what is mine and declare it to you" (John 16:14–15). Therefore, we should seek the Spirit's guidance as we give heed to the Word and should expect his help as we do so.

The promise of the Spirit's presence does not mean that the Scriptures will always be easy to understand. If understanding the Scriptures were a simple matter, we would not need divine assistance. The very fact that Jesus promises a divine Helper shows us that our human minds, influenced by many prejudices and sins, will often err as we seek to know the mind of Christ. Furthermore, living in these postmodern times when people are growing disillusioned with any hope of knowing truth, it is easy for Christians to succumb to the same despair and wonder whether it is even possible to understand the Scriptures. The Spirit's presence does not relieve us of the responsibility to wrestle in prayer over God's Word, but the promise of his presence assures us that attendance to preaching and Bible study is worthwhile. As Jesus brought us the words of the Father, so the Spirit will guide and support us in our ongoing response to those words.

We should expect the Spirit's help, therefore, in our study of Scripture. But we should expect his help as we search the Scriptures in communion with other believers, not simply as loners. Jesus used the plural form of the pronoun "you" when he promised that "the Spirit of truth . . . will guide you into all the truth" (16:13). In fact, in all of his references to the Spirit's teaching and explaining ministry, Jesus consistently used the plural "you." This means that *we should expect the Spirit to guide Christians as a community*. No one person can claim to have the Spirit in a way that makes his own interpretation the last word

THE PRACTICAL TRINITY 89

(2 Pet. 1:20). It is important for us to study our Bibles with confidence that the Spirit will help us, and to do so with careful attention to the counsel of others who have studied the same Scripture.

Preaching, sound Christian books, and the historic confessions and creeds of the church are all excellent ways to glean from the spiritual study of others in the community of faith. It is helpful to think of the church's confessions (like the Westminster Confession of Faith) as "Bible study notes" from past generations. Such documents are not produced to replace Scripture but have been prepared with a conviction that the Spirit guides the church, as a community, into a right understanding of the Word. Such documents may include errors. Jesus never promised that the Spirit would guarantee the church's infallibility. Nevertheless, following the examples of the New Testament apostles (e.g., Gal. 2:2; Acts 15), we respond to the Spirit's work by studying Scripture in community—in community with other believers today (in worship and Bible studies) and in community with Christians across the ages (taking counsel from the creeds and confessions).

The Spirit does more than help us respond to Christ's words, however. He also helps us carry Christ's words to others. "When the Helper comes," Jesus said, ". . . he will bear witness about me. And you also will bear witness . . ." (John 15:26–27; cf. 16:8–11). *The sending of the Spirit authorizes us to serve as witnesses.* Wherever Christians live, the Spirit is with them to make them witnesses to their communities.

In the Old Testament period, the witness of God's people was located in one country around one centralized temple. The temple priests were anointed at the beginning of their service in the temple (Exod. 29:7; 30:30). The anointing was a symbol of their being filled with the Spirit. But in the Old Testament era it was only in the temple that a full and authorized witness to the work of redemption was provided. The New Testament outpouring of the Spirit on all believers introduces a radical expansion of this gospel witness. The true drama of Pentecost was not the supernatural marks that accompanied it but the appointing of *all* believers for authoritative witness. Rather than bringing people to one central place of worship to repent with a sacrifice and to be enrolled by circumcision into the community of faith, the Spirit's descent has launched the church into the world, authorizing assemblies of believers everywhere for Spirit-empowered witness-bearing.

As the book of Acts shows us, evangelism is not always easy. Acts shows us examples of persecution, imprisonment, and many who refused the gospel as it was proclaimed to them. Having the Spirit authorizing and empowering us for witness does not mean that evangelism is easy or that people always believe. What it does mean, however, is that wherever Christians do bear witness, "as many as [are] appointed to eternal life [will] believe" (Acts 13:48). The Spirit authorizes believers to be evangelists, and he empowers their witness.

One final implication of the Spirit's role in the Christian's life should be noted. Jesus teaches us that it is the Spirit who remains "with [us] forever" (John 14:16), ministering the Father's purposes as accomplished by the Son. *We further respond to the continual presence of the Spirit by welcoming his conviction.* When we lack faith, the Spirit stirs our hearts to believe at the hearing of Scripture. When we sin, the Spirit brings conviction and draws our hearts to remember and obey the words of Scripture. When we are at odds with other people, it is the Spirit who confronts bitterness and applies the love of Christ to our conflicts. When we are struggling to obey God in the face of temptation, it is the Spirit who ministers grace to sustain us in obedience: "The fruit of the Spirit is love, joy, peace, patience, kindness, goodness, faithfulness, gentleness, self-control" (Gal. 5:22–23).

God's call to love and holiness would be overwhelming, and our frequent failures discouraging, if Jesus had left us to apply his teachings by ourselves. It is the promise of the Spirit that gives us encouragement in our struggles against sin and in our service for Christ. John Owen wrote, "Whilst Christ was in the world with his disciples, he made them no greater promise . . . [for] their own good [and for] carrying on the work which he had committed to them, than this of giving them the Holy Ghost . . . so that the whole religion we profess without the administration of the Spirit is nothing; nor is there any fruit without it."[7] We have daily reason, therefore, to give praise to God the Holy Spirit for his gracious and active work in our lives.

THE COMMUNION OF THE SAINTS

Jesus' Upper Room Discourse is packed with lessons on relationships. Jesus speaks about the relationships between himself, the Father, and the Spirit. Jesus also speaks about the relationships between each Person of the Godhead and the Christian and how all Three work together in God's communion with us. But we would miss an important facet of Jesus' instruction if we failed to address one final application from this doctrine of the Trinity—*our relationships with other Christians.*

Jesus talks in his discourse about our relationships with other Christians as an inseparable part of our communion with the triune God. The call to love one another was on Jesus' heart at the *beginning* of his Upper Room Discourse when he washed the disciples' feet and said, "I have given you an example, that you also should do just as I have done to you" (John 13:15). The call to love one another was on Jesus' heart at the *center* point of his discourse when he said, "These things I command you, so that you will love one another" (15:17). And Jesus still had this desire on his heart at the *end* of his discourse when he prayed to the Father, saying, "I do not ask for these only, but also for those who will believe in me through their word, that they may all be one, just as you, Father, are in me, and I in you, that they also may be in us" (17:20–21). We cannot rightly think about so heavenly

---

[7] Owen, *Of Communion with God the Father, Son, and Holy Ghost,* 254.

a topic as the Trinity without coming to as down-to-earth an application as loving one another.

From all eternity, the three Persons have enjoyed perfect love within the Godhead. When it pleased God to make mankind in his own image, he created us as social beings. We were created for relationship with God and to reflect his likeness not merely as individuals but in relationship with one another. This may be why the author of Genesis dared to use plural pronouns to describe God at that point in the creation account where he tells of God's creating mankind in his own likeness: "Then God said, 'Let *us* make man in *our* image, after *our* likeness.' . . . So God created man in his own image . . . male and female he created them" (Gen. 1:26–27).[8] God made man a social being because the prototype for man—God himself—is a being in communion.

In his Upper Room Discourse, Jesus is teaching us about the triune work of redemption as a work that renews men and women into right communion with God, and consequently into right communion with one another. While many aspects of the Trinity will always remain mysterious, Jesus explains enough about the Trinity to bring practical benefit to our Christian lives. As believers, we are called to meditate on the three Persons of the Godhead and to grow in our relationship with God in the ways examined in the preceding pages.

Jesus concluded his Upper Room Discourse with a prayer. In the final lines of that prayer, he shows that the perfection of the communion between God and his people will make heaven a joyful experience. "Father," Jesus prayed, "I desire that they also, whom you have given me, may be with me where I am. . . . I made known to them your name, and I will continue to make it known, that the love with which you have loved me may be in them, and I in them" (John 17:24–26). What a blessing! Jesus here promises "to continue to make [the Father's name and purposes]

---

[8] Cf. the discussion of this passage on pp 56–57 of this book.

known" to us. It is as Jesus continues to make the Father known to us through the ministry of the Holy Spirit among us that we are being sanctified in love and prepared for heaven.

May our Lord continue to teach us the nature of the triune God, granting us a foretaste of heavenly joy in our experience of his love now and preparing us for the fullness of that delight in eternity!

4

THE JOYOUS TRINITY

OUR TRIUNE GOD AND HIS PEOPLE

*Now when all the people were baptized, and when Jesus
also had been baptized and was praying, the heavens
were opened, and the Holy Spirit descended on him in
bodily form, like a dove; and a voice came from heaven,
"You are my beloved Son; with you I am well pleased."
(Luke 3:21–22)*

*Laud and honor to the Father,
Laud and honor to the Son,
Laud and honor to the Spirit,
Ever Three and ever One,
One in might, and One in glory,
While unending ages run.
(Trinity Hymnal, #343)*

✛

Augustine of Hippo is the author of one of the most profound
books ever written on the doctrine of the Trinity, *De Trinitate*.
According to legend, Augustine was walking by the sea one day
when he met a small boy pouring sea water into a hole in the
sand. Augustine asked the boy what he was doing. "Pouring the
sea into this hole," he said. "It will never fit," the great theologian
told the boy, "You're wasting your time!" "And so are you," the
boy shot back, "trying to write a book about God!"[1]

---

[1]Timothy George recounts a version of this story in *God the Holy Trinity: Reflections on
Christian Faith and Practice* (Grand Rapids, MI: Baker, 2006), 109.

Yet Augustine did write a classic book about the triune God, and in it he wrote:

> The Father, and the Son, and the Holy Spirit intimate a divine unity of one and the same substance in an indivisible equality; and therefore that they are not three Gods, but one God: although the Father hath begotten the Son, and so He who is the Father is not the Son; and the Son is begotten by the Father, and so He who is the Son is not the Father; and the Holy Spirit is neither the Father nor the Son, but only the Spirit of the Father and of the Son, Himself also co-equal with the Father and the Son, and pertaining to the unity of the Trinity.[2]

This is the way a theologian describes the doctrine of the Trinity, but how would an evangelist say it? The Gospel of Luke is a good place for us to explore the internal relationships within the triunity of God's being. Although the book is mainly about Jesus, at certain crucial junctures it reveals the triune God. Luke does not show us the Son only, but also the Father and the Spirit in their Trinitarian relationship with the Son.

THE BAPTISM

Consider what was done and said at Jesus' baptism: "Now when all the people were baptized, and when Jesus also had been baptized and was praying, the heavens were opened, and the Holy Spirit descended on him in bodily form, like a dove; and a voice came from heaven, 'You are my beloved Son; with you I am well pleased'" (Luke 3:21–22).

Luke seems to be less interested in the baptism itself—in fact, he does not even describe how the baptism took place or the person who performed it—than he was in what happened afterward. What attracted Luke's attention was the revelation of God in his triune being. All three Persons of the Trinity were present at this baptism—Father, Son, and Holy Spirit.

---

[2]Augustine, *On the Trinity*, 1.4.7, quoted in Philip Schaff, *Nicene and Post-Nicene Fathers*, First Series, 14 vols. (1886; repr. Peabody, MA: Hendrickson, 1994), 3:20.

Whenever God does anything important—which in one way or another includes everything he has ever done—it is the work of the entire Trinity. Here we see Trinitarian cooperation in action. God the Son (the Second Person of the Trinity) was praying. God the Holy Spirit (the Third Person of the Trinity) descended from heaven. And God the Father (the First Person of the Trinity) pronounced his benediction on the Son. The Son prayed, the Spirit descended, and the Father spoke.

When Jesus prayed, his prayers were answered, for the Spirit of God came down from heaven with a word from God. First, Luke says, "the heavens were opened" (v. 21). This was true in a literal sense. The clouds were parted and the skies sundered by the hand of God. But this phrase also refers to divine revelation. Whenever the Bible says that the heavens were opened, it means that the God of heaven revealed himself to his people on earth.

The descent of the dove does not mean that Jesus did not yet have the Spirit. We know that he did; the whole gospel is full of the Spirit. Jesus was conceived by the Spirit's power (Luke 1:35) and was filled with the Spirit's wisdom (Luke 2:40). But at his baptism, the Spirit made a public declaration that he was with Jesus for ministry. We see the implications of this all the way through the Gospels. It was by the power of the Holy Spirit that Jesus resisted temptation (Luke 4:1), preached the kingdom of God (Luke 4:14, 18), worshipped his Father in heaven (Luke 10:21), and performed mighty miracles (Matt. 12:28). It was also by the Spirit that he offered his body on the cross for our sins (Heb. 9:14) and was raised to give us eternal life (Rom. 1:4). Jesus did not do all these things independently, by his own intrinsic power, but dependently, by the power of the Holy Spirit. This intra-Trinitarian connection was publicly demonstrated and divinely validated at his baptism in the descent of the dove.

THE FATHER'S BLESSING

Then the Father spoke his word of blessing. This is the climax of the passage—the exaltation of Christ as the only Son of God. Luke shows that this is the climax by making the speaking of God's voice in verse 22 the main verb. The most important thing in this passage is what the Father said about the Son. Everything else is subordinate to his declaration: "You are my beloved Son; with you I am well pleased" (Luke 3:22). The Father said this in an audible voice so that people could hear what he was saying. He wanted everyone to know that Jesus Christ is his eternal Son—the mightiest one of all. This is one of the only times in the Gospels when the Father speaks with an audible voice, and when he does, it is to declare that Jesus is his beloved and well-pleasing Son.

The Father used two words to describe his relationship to the Son—a word of affection and a word of approval. The word of affection is "beloved." The Son is beloved by the Father, and this is their eternal relationship. The Greek word used here is *agapetos*, which generally means "beloved." However, when it is applied to a son or a daughter, it also means "only."[3] So the Father was declaring Jesus to be his Son in a unique sense: he is God the eternal Son, the only begotten of the Father. The Father loves to declare that Jesus is his Son, the Son whom he loves.

This expression of the Father's love for the Son rings with echoes from the Old Testament. It sounds similar to the way God spoke about Abraham's love for Isaac, his only son by God's promise (see Gen. 22:2, 12, 16). It also echoes God's declaration to Israel's king, and ultimately to Israel's Messiah, in Psalm 2: "You are my Son; today I have begotten you" (v. 7). Then there is Isaiah's prophecy: "Behold my servant, whom I uphold, my chosen, in whom my soul delights" (Isa. 42:1).

There is something special about a father's affection for his children. Until a man becomes a father, he may never realize how

---

[3] I. Howard Marshall, *The Gospel of Luke*, New International Greek Testament Commentary (Grand Rapids, MI: Eerdmans, 1978), 156.

beautiful a son or daughter can be. Then when his first child is born, he holds the child on his lap and says in his heart, "You are my beloved!"

This is also what God the Father said to Jesus Christ: "You are my beloved Son" (Luke 3:22). This does not mean that Jesus was not the Son before that time. On the contrary, his sonship is eternal. The Father was not performing some new act of adoption but was simply declaring on earth what had always been true in heaven. Only the Father could declare Jesus to be the one and only eternal Son of his love. This is the paternal affection at the heart of the Godhead. In his eternal sonship, the Son of God is loved by the Father.

Here is a great mystery. What can it mean for God to be loved by God? Within the inward relations of the Trinity we see the most perfect of all affections. The one who loves—in this case, the Father—loves with a perfect love. His affection knows no imperfection. And the one who is loved—in this case, the Son—is perfectly worthy to be loved. Thus there can be no more perfect love than the Father's love for his beloved Son within the Trinity.

With the Father's expression of affection came a word of approval: "with you I am well pleased" (Luke 3:22). There is always something precious about a father's approval. Is anything more important for a son than to have his father's blessing? Notice the precise wording of what the Father said to the Son: "with *you* I am well pleased." The very person of the Son pleased the Father. The Son was pleasing to the Father just because he was the Son. But the Father was also pleased with the Son's obedience. By submitting to baptism, Jesus was choosing to take the part of sinful humanity. He was agreeing to carry out the great task the Father had given him: to suffer and to die for sinners. So the Father blessed him.

The smile of fatherly approval rested on Jesus all the days of his life. As the Son did the work of our salvation, the Father was

pleased with everything he did. He was pleased with his obedience to his parents. He was pleased with his resistance to temptation. He was pleased with his teaching and his miraculous deeds
of mercy. He was pleased with his life of prayer. He was pleased
most of all with the sinless sacrifice that he offered on the cross.
We know this because he raised Jesus from the dead, which was
the ultimate proof of his approval. The Father was pleased with
all of it. He was pleased with what Jesus had done, was doing,
and would do. The Father took pleasure in the person and work
of his Son. The empty tomb is the proof of the Father's affection
and his approval for his beloved only Son.

The good news of the gospel is that if we believe in Jesus
Christ for our salvation, then God is just as pleased with us. The
Father's words of affection and approval are for his Son *and* for
everyone who has faith in his Son. This is what Jesus came to do:
to bring us into the Father's love. The things that we do are not
pleasing to God. If we had to stand before God the Father on
our own merits, we would never gain his approval or deserve his
affection. But we do not stand before God on our own merits.
As soon as we trust in Jesus Christ for our salvation, we stand
before the Father on the merits of his Son. Now he looks on us
with the same affection and approval that he has for Jesus Christ,
his worthy Son.

This is our hope when we are lonely or needy or fearful or
anxious or burdened by the great weight of our sin. It is our joy
when we feel that no one has ever really loved us the way we
long to be loved. No matter who we are or what we have done,
God is not unloving or disapproving but says to every one of his
children, "You are my beloved; with you I am well pleased!"

THE TRANSFIGURATION

Luke gives us another glimpse of affection and approval within
the Trinity when he shows us Jesus' transfiguration. Three disciples went up the mountain with Jesus, and there they both

saw and heard the glory of the Son as revealed by the Spirit and declared by the Father.

Here it is hard not to envy the disciples. Rather than simply reading the Gospels, as we do, the disciples lived them. When Jesus healed the sick and calmed the storm, they were there to see it. They were the first ones to learn the Lord's Prayer, the first to puzzle over his parables, and the first to learn everything else that Jesus had to teach. They were present when Jesus suffered his passion, returned from the grave, and ascended to heaven. The disciples were there when Jesus made redemptive history.

Sometimes it is tempting to think that the disciples had a relationship with Jesus that we could never experience or that somehow it was easier for them to carry the cross of discipleship. We may not covet their sufferings for the gospel, but sometimes we wish we could have walked in their sandals beside Jesus. And of all the things the apostles witnessed, none was more spectacular than their vision of the glorified Christ.

This glorious encounter began with a private retreat for prayer. It was no ordinary prayer meeting because "as he [Jesus] was praying, the appearance of his face was altered, and his clothing became dazzling white" (Luke 9:29). The disciples had only ever seen Jesus in the weakness of his flesh, which was part of the humiliation of his incarnation. As they went up the mountain, they saw him, as they always had, under the veil of his ordinary humanity. But then in a single instant, in a flash of time, Jesus was revealed to them in his divine splendor.

A VISION OF GLORY

What exactly did the apostles see? In what can only be described as a serious understatement, Luke says that "the appearance of his face was altered" (Luke 9:29). Matthew says more, telling us that Jesus "was transfigured before them, and his face shone like the sun" (Matt. 17:2). His appearance was not simply "altered" but "transfigured." In other words, it was illuminated with glory.

Peter, James, and John saw a blinding display of light, as if they were caught in the high beams of heaven. Jesus radiated with divine incandescence, his deity shining through the veil of his humanity. As the disciples gazed into his face, they saw a radiant luminescence that revealed the glory of God's Son.

As the disciples gazed upon this glorious revelation, they were seeing the glory that the Son had with the Father before the world began (John 17:5)—the eternal splendor of his divine being. They were seeing a visible manifestation of God's invisible glory. Here, for the first time in the Gospels, they were witnessing the majesty of God the Son, the Second Person of the Trinity. As Luke puts it, "they saw his glory" (Luke 9:32).

The disciples also heard something: "As he [Peter] was saying these things, a cloud came and overshadowed them, and they were afraid as they entered the cloud. And a voice came out of the cloud, saying, 'This is my Son, my Chosen One; listen to him!'" (Luke 9:34–35). Here was an even greater manifestation of divine glory. The disciples had seen the person of Jesus shining in splendor, but now a glorious cloud came down out of heaven from God to envelop Jesus and the prophets and possibly also the disciples themselves.

This glory-cloud made the disciples tremble with fear, and well it should, because it was nothing less than the glory of God. The disciples were seeing what Moses saw when God descended on the tabernacle (Exod. 40:34–35), what Solomon saw when God's presence filled Israel's house of worship (2 Chron. 7:1–3), and what Ezekiel saw rising from the temple on the wings of the cherubim (Ezek. 10:3–5). They were seeing the glory of Almighty God—his *Shekinah* glory, in Hebrew terminology—the radiant cloud that gave people a visible manifestation of his invisible majesty.

The cloud alone would have been enough to confirm God's presence and blessing. But God also spoke. It was of course *his* voice that came from the cloud, and he knew exactly what he was talking about. The divine voice identified Jesus as his Son and chosen One, the One to whom the disciples must listen. God may have said this partly to encourage Jesus in his preparation for the cross. Just as the Father spoke at the Son's baptism (see Luke 3:22), so now again at the transfiguration, as the Son is on his way to Calvary, the Father speaks to confirm the Son's calling as his chosen servant. However, what God said was mainly for the benefit of the disciples and for us. People had long speculated about the true identity of Jesus. The disciples themselves were beginning to confess him as the Christ, without fully understanding what this meant. But here now was an authoritative revelation from God. Who is Jesus? He is the chosen Son of God.

What God said to Peter, James, and John needs to be understood against the background of the Old Testament. When God called Jesus his Son, this reflected their eternal relationship within the triune being of God. There is only one God, and this one God exists in three Persons—the Father, the Son, and the Holy Spirit. Jesus Christ is God the eternal Son. Surely this is part of what the Father meant when he declared Jesus to be his Son.

Yet the sonship of Jesus Christ refers also to his kingship. In the Old Testament psalms of David, God sometimes spoke to the king of Israel as his son: "You are my Son; today I have begotten you. Ask of me, and I will make the nations your heritage, and the ends of the earth your possession" (2:7–8). Therefore, when God the Father calls Jesus his Son, he is granting him a royal title—a title that testifies to his kingly authority. God glorified Jesus as his royal and eternal Son.

When God speaks, people should listen. Here, in the space of just a few short words, God speaks volumes of sacred truth about the person and work of Jesus Christ. Jesus is God's royal and eternal Son, the chosen servant of our salvation, the prophet who speaks the truth of God. It is no wonder that he was transfigured in glory! The Father was glorifying Jesus as the Son of everlasting glory, as the King who rules us, as the Savior who died for us, and as the prophet who teaches us everything we need to know.

Some people say they would be willing to listen to Jesus if only he would speak to them in an audible voice. They want God to speak to them *directly*. If only they could hear what Peter and the other disciples heard on the mountain, if only they could see what they saw, then they would believe!

The apostle Peter himself wrote about this experience in his second epistle: "We were eyewitnesses of his majesty. For when he received honor and glory from God the Father, and the voice was borne to him by the Majestic Glory, 'This is my beloved Son, with whom I am well pleased,' we ourselves heard this very voice borne from heaven, for we were with him on the holy mountain" (2 Pet. 1:16–18). That is all very well for Peter, but what about us? Of course, we take Peter's word for it that these things really happened, but how does that help us if we never have the same mountaintop experience?

Peter went on to make this remarkable comment: "And we have something more sure, the prophetic word, to which you will do well to pay attention as to a lamp shining in a dark place, until the day dawns and the morning star rises in your hearts" (v. 19). According to Peter, what the Scripture says about Jesus is even more certain than what he heard and saw on the mountain. The gospel is more complete; it contains everything we need to know about Jesus, not just the glorious glimpse that the disciples were given. It is also more permanent. What Peter experienced on the mountain only lasted for a little while, but God's Word is eternal. Whenever we have any questions about Jesus, or about the true way of salvation, or about what God wants us to do, we can go back to the Bible again and again.

When we pay attention to what the Bible says about Jesus, we see his glory for ourselves. Peter says that faith in Christ is like the rising of the morning star. In other words, it is like the planet Venus—the morning star—rising in all its beauty on a clear morning, piercing the dusky horizon with its steady gleam. This is what it is like when we listen to Jesus and look to him for our salvation. The glorious Son of God gives us the eternal light and beauty and joy of the triune God.

THE FIRST MISSION TRIP

Joy is also the mood in Luke 10, when the first gospel missionaries returned from their first mission trip. Jesus sent seventy-two evangelists out to heal the sick and to proclaim, "The kingdom of God has come near to you" (v. 9). When they had fulfilled their mission, "The seventy-two returned with joy, saying, 'Lord, even the demons are subject to us in your name!'" (v. 17). The seventy-two evangelists were celebrating the great joy of God's victory over Satan.

As much exuberant joy as they had in their triumph over Satan, Jesus told his servants that something else should give them even greater joy—the promise of eternal life. "Nevertheless," he said, "do not rejoice in this, that the spirits are subject to you, but rejoice that your names are written in heaven" (v. 20). This does not mean that we should not rejoice in what we do in ministry, of course. But this is a superior joy—knowing that our names are written in the Book of Life.

Sometime late in 1980 Iain Murray visited the aging Dr. Martyn Lloyd-Jones. The famous London preacher was drawing near to death and could only sit up for an hour or two each day. Murray asked an obvious question: "How are you coping now that your ministry is so confined?" After all, Lloyd-Jones had preached to countless thousands, bringing many to faith in Christ. He had also had a leading role in establishing important evangelical institutions like Tyndale House, The Westminster Conference, and The Banner of Truth. Lloyd-Jones replied, "Do not rejoice that the demons are subject to you in my name, but rejoice that your name is written in heaven." Then he said, "I am perfectly content." This is the deepest source of the believer's joy through life and on into eternity: our salvation is not based on what we have done but on God's saving grace, for our names are written in the Book of Life.[4]

Is any joy greater than knowing we have eternal life? Yes, in fact there is a greater joy—the greatest joy of all—the joy that God the Son has in God the Spirit and God the Father. Luke tells us, "In that same hour he rejoiced in the Holy Spirit and said, 'I thank you, Father, Lord of heaven and earth . . .'" (10:21).

The word that Luke uses here for rejoicing is more exalted than any other word for joy, including the other words he has used in this very passage. The Greek word *agalliao* is a word for exuberant ecstasy, for complete exultation in the fullness of joy. And when we see why Jesus was rejoicing, we can understand why Luke used it here. Jesus rejoiced to see Satan defeated and to give us the free gift of eternal life. But here was an even greater joy because it took place within the triune being of God, who exists eternally as one God in three Persons.

By its very nature, the joy of Jesus is greater than any joy that we could ever experience. Because Jesus is God the Son, his joy is a divine rejoicing. It is a perfect joy, unspoiled and undiminished by sin. But here his joy is especially intense because he is rejoicing in the revelation of the Holy Spirit and in the secret, saving work of his Father. Luke is showing us the joy at the heart of the universe, the rejoicing that takes place within the Godhead, where God is both the subject and the object of his own joy. The Father, the Son, and the Spirit glory in one another. When Jesus was baptized (Luke 3:22), and again when he was transfigured (Luke 9:35), we saw the pleasure the Father takes in his own beloved Son. Here Jesus rejoices in the Spirit and in the Father, and as he rejoices, we catch a glimpse of God glorifying and enjoying himself.

There can be no greater joy than this: the reciprocal and eternal joy that God himself enjoys in the being of God. God's chief

---

[4]This story was related in personal correspondence from D. A. Carson to Philip Ryken.

end is to glorify himself and enjoy himself forever. On this occasion, Jesus was so overwhelmed with triune joy that in a spontaneous outburst he rejoiced out loud. He rejoiced in the Holy Spirit, finding his enjoyment in the Third Person of the Trinity. He also rejoiced in the Father, praising him for his supreme greatness over heaven and earth.

WHY JESUS REJOICED

Many people would be surprised at the occasion for this joy. Why was Jesus rejoicing? Because, he said to his Father, "you have hidden these things from the wise and understanding and revealed them to little children; yes, Father, for such was your gracious will" (Luke 10:21–22). Jesus was rejoicing over the sovereignty of God in salvation, over the doctrine of election, over the fact that God only reveals the truths of salvation to his own beloved children.

People often consider the sovereignty of God's grace to be a dark and difficult doctrine. Why does God bring some people to a saving knowledge of Jesus Christ, while others are left to perish in their sins? The Bible never gives us the full answer, except to say that God does it for his own glory. But far from treating this mystery as an occasion for anxiety, the Bible presents it as a comfort for the soul. The doctrine of election, which proves God's sovereignty in salvation, is a doctrine of joy. We find this on Christmas night, when the angels sang, "Glory to God in the highest!" and blessed the people who are under God's pleasure (Luke 2:14). We find it in Romans 9–11, where Paul's exposition of election ends with a grand doxology of praise. We find it in Ephesians 1, where the fact that God has chosen us in Christ is celebrated with high praise to God. We also find it here in Luke 10, where God's sovereignty in salvation brings joy to the very Godhead.

Jesus rejoices in the Father's gracious will to reveal salvation to some but not to others. To be specific, God has hidden the secrets of his gospel from people who think they are wise and revealed them instead to "little children" (literally, "to babies")— in other words, to people who know that they do not know everything and who therefore come to him in simple, childlike faith.

When Jesus spoke about "the wise and understanding," he may well have been referring to members of the religious establishment, such as the Pharisees and the Sadducees—theological know-it-alls who refused to believe that he was the Christ. When he spoke about "little children," he was referring to his ordinary disciples, who for all their weakness were learning to follow him in faith and obedience. It is not ignorance that Jesus is praising here but humility. Norval Geldenhuys has rightly observed that the contrast is

> not that between "educated" and "uneducated" but between those who imagine themselves to be wise and sensible and want to test the Gospel truths by their own intellects and to pronounce judgment according to their self-formed ideas and those who live under the profound impression that by their own insight and their own reasoning they are utterly powerless to understand the truths of God and to accept them.[5]

If we are wise, therefore, we will accept the biblical teaching about God, which includes the doctrine of the Trinity—that there is one God in three Persons. We will receive the great mystery of the Trinity with childlike faith and joyful praise.

As Jesus rejoiced in the Spirit, he went on to say, "All things have been handed over to me by my Father, and no one knows who the Son is except the Father, or who the Father is except the Son and anyone to whom the Son chooses to reveal him" (Luke 10:22). In verse 21 he had rejoiced in the revelation of the Father; here he rejoices in his own revelation as the Son. It is all interconnected. Jesus Christ is God the Son. Therefore, everything that

---

[5]Norval Geldenhuys, *Luke*, New International Commentary on the New Testament (Grand Rapids, MI: Eerdmans, 1951), 306–307.

belongs to the Father—such as his sovereign power and divine authority—also belongs to the Son.

When Jesus said that the Father had given him all things, he was making the strongest possible claim to his own deity. All things belong to Jesus Christ, the Son of God. Not a single subatomic particle in the entire universe is outside his supreme lordship. Due to his divine identity, the Son has perfect knowledge of the Father, in the same way that the Father has perfect knowledge of the Son. The Father and the Son share mutual intimacy with the Spirit in the fellowship of their triune being. Only God can know God perfectly, and therefore no one knows the Son like the Father, or the Father like the Son.

And yet—this is the reason Jesus rejoices—we ourselves are able to have fellowship with the triune God. By the grace of the Father, according to the will of the Son, through the revelation of the Holy Spirit, we know the living God. It is the work of the Son to bring us into fellowship with the Father, and Jesus rejoices that this is so. David Gooding writes, "As Son of the Father he enjoyed unique knowledge of the intimate relationship that lies at the heart of the Godhead, and with that unique knowledge the unique privilege of communicating it to whomever he pleased."[6] However, it is not just the knowledge of God that Jesus communicates to us, but also the joy of God. God the Son came into the world so that we could enter his joy—the joy of knowing and loving the Godhead.

OUR COMMISSION

The glorious joy of the Godhead is meant to be shared. To see this, we need to consider one more fully Trinitarian moment in the Gospel of Luke:

> Then he said to them, "These are my words that I spoke to you while I was still with you, that everything written about

[6]David Gooding, *According to Luke: A New Exposition of the Third Gospel* (Grand Rapids, MI: Eerdmans, 1987), 202.

me in the Law of Moses and the Prophets and the Psalms must be fulfilled." Then he opened their minds to understand the Scriptures, and said to them, "Thus it is written, that the Christ should suffer and on the third day rise from the dead, and that repentance and forgiveness of sins should be proclaimed in his name to all nations, beginning from Jerusalem. You are witnesses of these things. And behold, I am sending the promise of my Father upon you. But stay in the city until you are clothed with power from on high." (Luke 24:44–49)

This is Luke's version of the Great Commission. Jesus had opened the minds of his disciples to understand the Scriptures—everything in the Old Testament. His instruction covered the whole work of the gospel: the cross, the resurrection, and then the mission of the church to take the gospel to the world. But notice especially how this commission ended—with the blessing of the Holy Spirit, who is called "the promise of my Father" (v. 49).

Though often overlooked, this is one of the most important Trinitarian passages in all of Scripture. Here we see the Son in all his saving power. Jesus is preaching his own Easter-day sermon, in which he proclaims himself as the Savior of the world: "Then he opened their minds to understand the Scriptures, and said to them, 'Thus it is written, that the Christ should suffer and on the third day rise from the dead'" (vv. 45–46). The gospel promise that was given in the Old Testament—the promise of the Christ—finds its fulfillment in Jesus and his saving work.

These were all things that Jesus had told his disciples before, that "The Son of Man must suffer many things . . . and be killed, and on the third day be raised" (Luke 9:22). Now he was saying these things to them again, from the far side of the cross and the empty tomb. He was preaching Christ crucified and Christ risen, Christ suffering and dying and rising again. He was preaching the gospel with a call to repentance and faith.

Then Jesus told the disciples, as he tells us, that this would now become *their* message—their gospel to the world. Repentance and the forgiveness of sins should be proclaimed to all nations. The apostles were eyewitness of the risen Christ, and thus it was their calling to bear witness to his saving grace around the world.

To carry out this mission, the disciples needed the power of the Third Person of the Trinity. So the Son would send the Spirit, who is the promise of the Father. In effect Jesus was giving his disciples a farewell gift. The parting gift that Jesus promised his friends is the best of all gifts. "And behold," he said to his disciples, "I am sending the promise of my Father upon you. But stay in the city until you are clothed with power from on high" (Luke 24:49). What Jesus meant by the "promise" of his Father was the Third Person of the Trinity—the Holy Spirit himself. With this unique and extraordinary parting gift, Jesus gave his disciples the very power of God. He also showed us the true relationship of the Father to the Spirit. Just as the Son is the beloved Son, so the Spirit is the promised Spirit.

The word "promise" is the perfect word to use in this regard because God had long promised to send his people the Spirit. In fact, the sending of the Spirit is one of the many things that Jesus said was written in the Scriptures (see Luke 24:44). The same Scriptures that said the Christ would die and rise again (Luke 24:46) and that promised the preaching of repentance and forgiveness to all nations (Luke 24:47) also said that God would pour out the Holy Spirit on his people.

There was a time, for example, when God took the Spirit who had already been with Moses and gave the same Spirit to the seventy elders also. When this happened, Moses said he wished that God would pour his Spirit out on all his people, not just on the elders (see Num. 11:29). This is exactly what the prophets promised. Isaiah prophesied that the Spirit would be "poured upon us from on high" (Isa. 32:15)—upon all the offspring of Jacob (Isa. 44:3). Ezekiel said that God would put his Spirit in people's hearts (Ezek. 36:27). Joel said that in the last days God would pour his Spirit on all his people—men and women, young and old (Joel 2:28–29; cf. Ezek. 39:29). Jesus promised the same thing when he said that the Father would send the Spirit in the name of the Son (John 14:16–17, 26). The gift of the Holy Spirit is the promise of God.

IN THE POWER OF THE SPIRIT

This gift is absolutely essential and totally necessary for any effective ministry. Jesus was sending the apostles out to be his witnesses to the world. As they preached repentance and forgiveness through the cross and the empty tomb, they would be utterly dependent on the work of the Holy Spirit. How could they ever fulfill their calling to reach the world for Christ in their own strength? Without the Spirit, not even the preaching of the gospel would have any effect on people, because faith in Jesus and repentance from sin are gifts of the Holy Spirit. No one ever comes to faith in Christ or knows God as Father without the Spirit's regenerating work. But praise God—Jesus has sent us the Spirit he promised to send! Jesus knew that we could never make it on our own; we need the power of God for ministry and for missions. We have that power by the presence and the work of the Holy Spirit. So our gospel does not come to people in words alone, "but also in power and in the Holy Spirit" (1 Thess. 1:5).

The gospel does this because Jesus fulfilled his promise, sending the Spirit on the day of Pentecost. With flames of fire and the rushing of a mighty wind, the Spirit was poured out on the church (see Acts 2:1–4, 33). The Holy Spirit has been with us ever since, clothing us with "power from on high" (Luke 24:49), just as Jesus promised. Now, by the gifts and graces of the Holy Spirit, even our own feeble efforts to share the gospel can bring people salvation. We do not need to be discouraged but may believe that whatever we do for Jesus is brought to its perfect end by the Holy Spirit, who is the power of the triune God.

This powerful gift happens to be the best gift that Jesus could possibly send us because it is the gift of God himself. Like the Father and the Son, the Spirit himself is divine. This makes Luke 24:49 one of the most strongly and completely Trinitarian verses in the entire Bible: "And behold, I am sending the promise of my Father upon you. But stay in the city until you are clothed with power from on high." This verse is spoken by God the Son with reference to both the Father and the Spirit. Jesus is telling us that the gift of the Spirit is sent from the Father and the Son. To receive this parting gift, therefore, is to receive the gift of the triune God himself.

What greater gift could God possibly give us than the gift of himself, in the Person of his Spirit? In giving us the Spirit, God is giving us himself in all his saving grace. To have the Spirit is to know the truth of God's Word, because the Spirit who inspired the Word also opens our minds and hearts to understand it. To have the Spirit is to know forgiveness, because the Spirit convicts the conscience and leads us to repent of our sin. To have the Spirit is to have eternal life, because the Spirit convinces us of the truth of the gospel and enables us to believe in Jesus Christ. To have the Spirit is to have God's comfort in every trial we suffer, because when Jesus said that he would be with us always (see Matt. 28:20), he was talking about the abiding presence of the Holy Spirit, who is the Comforter of God (see John 14:16). To have the Spirit is also to have grace for personal sanctification and power for Christian witness.

Have you received the gift of the Holy Spirit? Every believer in Jesus Christ has the Holy Spirit, for to receive Christ is to receive his Spirit. But if you have not trusted in Christ and do not have this gift or are not certain whether you have it or not, all you need to do is ask. God has promised to give his Spirit to anyone who asks in faith (see Luke 11:13).

If you *have* received the Holy Spirit, be sure to thank God for the best of all gifts—the one gift that brings you all the blessings of the triune God. Without the Spirit you would never believe the Bible. Without the Spirit you would never confess your sins.

Without the Spirit you would never know Jesus for sure. Without the Spirit you would never receive eternal life. The Holy Spirit is the fullness of the Godhead. When he makes his home within us, glory comes down, and we are filled with gratitude to the Triune God—Father, Son, and Holy Spirit.

This is perhaps the best place for us to end our study of the Trinity—with gratitude to the Godhead. Theologian Eric Mascall insisted that the Trinity is never merely a doctrine but always meant to be a grateful joy. To say that God is triune, he wrote, is to say that "there are three divine persons eternally united in one life of complete perfection and beatitude." This tri-union "is the secret of God's most infinite life and being, into which, in his infinite love and generosity, he has admitted us, and is therefore to be accepted with amazed and exultant gratitude."[7] So may God give us joyful amazement and eternal gratitude for the glorious mystery of his triune being!

---

[7]Eric Mascall, quoted in Peter Toon, *Yesterday, Today, and Forever* (Swedesboro, NJ: Preservation, 1996), 210.

SCRIPTURE INDEX

SUBJECT INDEX